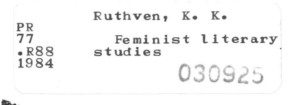

Feminist literary studies

Feminist literary studies:
an introduction

K. K. RUTHVEN
University of Adelaide, Australia

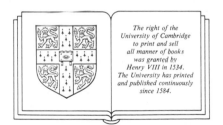

*The right of the
University of Cambridge
to print and sell
all manner of books
was granted by
Henry VIII in 1534.
The University has printed
and published continuously
since 1584.*

CAMBRIDGE UNIVERSITY PRESS

Cambridge
London   New York   New Rochelle
Melbourne   Sydney

Published by the Press Syndicate of the University of Cambridge
The Pitt Building, Trumpington Street, Cambridge CB2 1RP
32 East 57th Street, New York, NY 10022, USA
10 Stamford Road, Oakleigh, Melbourne 3166, Australia

First published 1984
Reprinted 1985, 1986

Printed in Great Britain at
the University Press, Cambridge

Library of Congress catalogue card number: 84–9592

British Library cataloguing in publication data

Ruthven, K. K.
Feminist literary studies.
1. English literature–History and
criticism   2. Feminism and literature
3. Women critics
I. Title
820.9'9287   PR65.W6

ISBN 0 521 26454 5 hard covers
ISBN 0 521 26998 9 paperback

GG

Contents

Preface

This book is based on seminars conducted with students who took the opportunity, in their final year of study for an Honours degree in English language and literature, to examine some influential styles of critical discourse developed over the last fifteen years or so, among them feminist criticism. The aim was to identify some characteristic features of various types of literary criticism which are called feminist, and to see how they relate not only to one another but also – by means of assimilation or opposition – to recent and current 'non-feminist' criticism. The book is written accordingly from inside English studies, and concerns itself with feminist ideologies only in so far as these result in literary critical practices which, collectively, constitute a major critique of 'Eng. Lit.' as an academic subject.

Part of chapter 1 was published in a somewhat different form in the October 1983 issue of *Essays in criticism*, and I am grateful to the editors of that journal for permission to reprint it.

K. K. RUTHVEN

February 1984

1

The gendering of critical discourse

Where to begin is always a problem when writing a book, but particularly a book about feminist criticism, especially if you happen to be a man. The reason for this is that feminist theory has politicised all the usual manoeuvres engaged in by men who write books about books, so that whatever they do is likely to be considered symptomatic of the problem of male domination to which feminists address themselves. If you are a man and you decide (as I have done) to take a look at feminist criticism, you may find yourself at risk from a feminist mode of cinematic discourse which categorises 'looking' as a morbid activity engaged in by men to the detriment of women, who are reduced consequently to mere objects of voyeuristic attention.[1] To want to 'look' at feminist criticism, therefore, is only what you would expect of a man in a male-dominated society, for in doing so he simply complies with the rules of a symbolic order of representation which displays women's ideas in the same way that films and girlie magazines display their bodies, and for the same purposes: vulgar curiosity and the arousal of desire.

Such modes of representation are sometimes called 'androcentric' because they are centred on men (Greek *andros*, 'male'), and sometimes 'phallocentric', partly because in most systems of sexual differentiation the phallus is taken to be the principal signifier of the male, and partly because of the special significance attached to it in psychoanalytic theory, the details of which I shall describe later. But in so far as possession of a phallus entails possession of power in a phallocentric society, the term used by most feminists to describe a symbolic order of representation which is also male-specific is 'phallocratic' (Greek *kratos*, 'power'). And the social system which corresponds to such a phallocratic order − a system which enables men to dominate women in all social relations − is known in feminist discourse as 'patriarchy', a term which some feminists find unhelpfully vague, but which continues to be used because no satisfactory

1

alternative is available. The oppressive effects of patriarchal domination manifest themselves as 'sexism'.

It is believed that in the phallocratic order of knowledge perpetuated in our patriarchal society, the kind of looking which results in 'knowing' is likely to be exploitative. For knowledge is treated as something quite separate from the knower, and as capable of being known 'objectively', provided the knower aspires to 'impersonality', separating self from object in order to give the self power over objects. Men see knowledge, in other words, as something to be 'mastered' in the way that women are to be mastered. And therefore any thoroughgoing critique of the phallocratic oppression of women must begin by recognising that the cult of so-called objective and impersonal modes of knowing makes what we call 'knowledge' complicit in that oppression. Any man who tries to 'master' the texts of feminism is guilty of replicating at the level of discourse those oppressive practices which enable men to subordinate and manipulate women. A passion for mastery results in the molestation or rape of whatever it subordinates: symbolically, it is a phallic activity, whether it is practised by men who do it 'naturally', or by women who can be trained to do it in a patriarchal system of education.

I mention such general objections to the writing of books by men on feminist topics because they function rhetorically to dissuade men from entering the debate on the grounds that they are somehow disqualified from doing so. This is a new experience for most men. And while it may be said that it will do them good to feel excluded for a change (because women have always felt excluded by non-feminist criticism) I think the long-term effects of exclusionism are bad. Literary criticism thrives on provocation and dissent, and its renovation depends on the discovery of new questions with which to interrogate books and ways of talking about them. Feminism is well stocked with such questions. But as the history of early Freudian criticism shows, people become impatient with the tactic of attempting to stifle dissent by claiming that objections to cherished theories and procedures are merely symptomatic of the problem (I am recalling the days when, unless you conceded the 'fact' that an umbrella is a phallic symbol, you could be accused of being too inhibited to notice such things). Given a false choice between being considered symptomatic and being silent, you have to opt for being considered symptomatic in order to make any critical remarks at all in what has been constructed as a no-win situation. The male explorer of feminist criticism is always falling into similar traps. Certain features of this discourse, for instance, have not yet been labelled, and therefore in thinking about them I am tempted to invent names for them – as French feminists do – so that they can be recognised and described. But to do so would be to slip once more into phallocratic bad habits, colonising the new space which women have made for themselves by sticking male signposts up all over the place. For as Mary Daly keeps reminding us, the power of naming was conferred by God on Adam but not on Eve, and in naming the animals Adam took dominion over them.[2] In Daly's terms, women will remain powerless until they themselves exercise the power of naming.

The tactic of attempting to discredit books like this before they ever get written is therefore one which I am obliged to ignore, for to capitulate to it would be to deny the possibility of saying anything at all about the nature and development of feminist criticism. If that seems an arbitrary attitude to adopt, it is worth remembering that this is what happens whenever criticism gets itself into an impasse, as most recently in the case of deconstruction. Instead of trying to theorise themselves out of trouble on such occasions, critics escape the consequences of their own arguments by resorting to a common sense which is widely disparaged nowadays at the highest levels of criticism. Books about deconstruction, for example, ought to be a contradiction in terms, in so far as deconstructionists claim that the duplicitous nature of language makes stable meanings impossible; but that has not prevented the publication of lucid accounts of deconstructionist theory and practice, a feat which can be achieved only by ignoring the language-scepticism which is so strikingly characteristic of deconstructionist criticism, and acting as if the figural indeterminacies which haunt the languages of literature and of criticism do not affect the language of 'metacriticism', the criticism of criticism.[3] Similarly, in order to proceed I am obliged to ignore those features of my own text which a feminist critique of it might deem phallocratic, such as its reduction of different kinds of feminist criticism to an ordered set of discursive positions. To act otherwise would involve writing a book about whether men can write books about feminist criticism. And who would want to read that, even if I could write it? In other words, although it is pertinent to raise questions of discourse and authority in connection with a book written by a man about a body of criticism produced mainly by women, I am not convinced that the question itself constitutes a wholly disabling objection to the procedure I follow here. Briefly, this is to look closely and critically at those critical theories and practices which are called feminist, and which were both focused and catalysed by the publication of Kate Millett's *Sexual politics* in 1970. As for the possibility that in doing so I risk being charged with hermeneutical rape, I take heart from Jane Gallop's observation that there are more ways than one to have intercourse with textual bodies, and that in the kind to which we should all, men as well as women, aspire, 'entry and interpenetration do not mean disrespect or violation'.[4]

ii

'Feminist literary criticism' is a familiar enough term: we use it all the time, but what does it mean? Each of its constituent words is highly problematic. For instance, to which of the many feminisms, ancient and modern, does 'feminist' refer? What does the word 'literary' mean, now that literature is said to be no longer the generic term for a diversity of texts bonded into a canon by an elusive property called 'literariness', but rather the product of categorising acts which result in some texts being declared 'literature' and others not – acts which serve some people's interests more than others', and are therefore political in nature? And as for 'criticism', is the word being used in the older sense of a variety of discursive practices subservient to the elucidation and evaluation of works of literature? Or is it being used in the newer sense of a discourse which uses literary texts – if at all – only as occasions which prompt further theorising, thus establishing criticism as a primary mode of writing like poetry and fiction, and not a merely 'secondary' commentary upon such allegedly primary modes? 'Feminist literary criticism', in other words, is a deceptively serene label for the contestations it identifies, and the turbulence created by the collocation of those three vexed words would be signalled much more clearly if we were to write it as 'feminist' 'literary' 'criticism'. But that would not solve the further problem of whether it should be kept as a separate entity attached to a particular subject-discipline (such as English studies) or whether it should be subsumed into the cross-disciplinary institution of 'feminist criticism', one of whose interests will continue to be literature for as long as literary studies last, but which is already prepared for the day – should it ever arrive – when literature is annexed by cultural studies and has to vie for attention alongside more popular signifying practices such as films and television.

The radical critique of literary studies which has been going on since the late 1960s has not been so successful as to support unequivocally the claim that the end is nigh, and that the study of literature (in the highbrow sense: Literature) is finished. Notoriously, the institution of literary studies copes with radical critiques of its activities by coming to terms with them. This is a residual problem for radical critics, who object to having their discourse 'appropriated' by the academy. The academy, however, claims to be merely 'accommodating' such discourses. Clearly, how you see it depends on where you are standing. Radicals oppose the academy and its practices as a manifestation of an establishment they want to see changed. But in so far as most radicals pass through the academy, and some end up employed there, they are bound to be treated by the academy, however reluctantly, as its avant-garde – prodigal sons and daughters whose outrageous goings-on result eventually in modifications to institutional practices, specifically in a revised view of what the object of enquiry ought to be and what might be the best ways of dealing with it.

As an institution, literary criticism develops and survives by such processes of accommodation. It is interested in the new rather as a means of transforming than supplanting the old. Its methodological incoherence is a scandal only to those who wish to replace it by something else, and who therefore seek out some 'central' set of assumptions which, if discredited, would bring the whole edifice tumbling down. But the institution of literary criticism tolerates a great variety of practices whose only relationship with one another is contiguity. Some practitioners are self-conscious about what they are doing, and others are not, but all have a sense – exaggerated in the eyes of some of the others – of their own importance, and work hard at refining their practices. The advent of the new affects some practices more than others and may result in intramural debates, often conducted in that highly articulate style of acrimony which literary people are particularly good at; but eventually the new gets accommodated somewhere in the system, and is tolerated by the rest to the extent that they stop objecting to it and get on with what they consider to be their own more worthwhile work. One of the reasons for this is that the new, like the old, is never a singularity but always an amalgam of diversities, different bits of which are likely to appeal to different parts of the institution which does the accommodating. The institution of criticism is not so much a fortress which feminists have to storm but rather a building with many apartments, the doors to some of which are open to some kinds of feminist. Nobody doubts the existence of a siege mentality towards any kind of feminism in certain quarters of the institution; but at the same time, it has to be conceded that some feminists, like some marxists, exaggerate the difficulties of their task in order to develop in one another a sense of heroic solidarity in the face of overwhelming odds.

How you see the relationship between feminist discourse and literature depends therefore on whether you believe feminism can or should be contained within the institution of literary studies. If it can, then our business is to learn from feminist criticism how to improve the study of English language and literature, specifically by removing from it those procedures which are vulnerable to a feminist critique, or modifying them (as in the case of canon-formation) in such a way as to take account of that critique. If it cannot, then nothing short of a cultural revolution will suffice, involving a total transformation of society and its institutions, including the academies. 'The feminist project is to end male domination', writes Andrea Dworkin. 'In order to do this, we will have to destroy the structure of culture as we know it, its art, its churches, its laws; its nuclear families based on father-right and nation-states; all of the images, institutions, customs, and habits which define women as worthless and invisible victims.'[5] But the prospects for a sexual revolution along the lines of China's short-lived cultural revolution are slight; and given that the appropriation/accommodation of feminist discourse by English studies is already under way, the relation of feminism to literary studies would seem obliged at the moment to take the form of negotiation rather than confrontation. It is going to be no more difficult for the academies to learn to live with feminism than it has been for them to learn to live with marxism.

The principal problem posed by the emergence of feminist literary criticism is the pedagogical one. For the majority of people in the teaching profession this comes down to determining the best way of accommodating the discourse of feminism into that babble of heterogeneous discourses created by traditional voices vying with newer accents. It may be objected, and rightly, that there is more to feminism than pedagogy, and that the aim of a feminist criticism as of any revolutionary criticism should be to subvert the dominant discourses, not to make compromises with them. Each of these observations, and others like them, could be taken as the starting-point for a very different kind of book from this one, which I have chosen to write partly because I lacked the inclination (and in some cases the ability) to write any of the others, and partly because the intervention of feminism in English studies – which is taught, problematically, largely by men largely to women – is an important moment in the history of feminism as well as in the history of English studies. It was never suggested to male teachers who completed their formal education before the late 1960s that feminism might be even remotely relevant to the teaching of English. The result was that when feminist criticism finally presented itself to men already in the profession it was construed as merely supplementary to what needed to be known. What was called (misleadingly) the 'feminist perspective' was imagined to be something which trendies would take up and troglodytes put down, and which the rest of us might mention from time to time if it seemed relevant to the interpretation of a particular text. But feminism claims to be much more than a perspective, and the growing volume, sophistication and acuteness of feminist literary criticism – together with its strategic alliance with the most disruptive critical theories of our time – have placed it at the centre of critiques of English studies as traditionally conceived. The feminist intervention strikes me as being incontestably the most important challenge faced by English studies in the twenty or more years I have been associated with it. This does not mean that I approve unreservedly of the way it goes about its business, for it is excessively fond of 'underdetermined' theories which impose a feminist interpretation on data which can be interpreted equally well by alternative and non-feminist theories. But I think men should be encouraged to engage in feminist criticism less self-consciously than they are obliged to do at present. 'If . . . feminist literary study has profoundly revolutionary implications for literary study as a whole', William W. Morgan remarked in a 1976 exchange with Annette Kolodny, 'then, in some sense, it's everybody's business.'[6] That strikes me as a responsible attitude to take, and one which all men in the teaching profession should adopt, provided they bear in mind Morgan's caveat and are careful to speak '*about* feminist literary thinkers and not *for* them'. Some women think even so small a liberty is excessive. So before proceeding further we should consider why they do so, and what grounds there are for opposing the exclusionist argument that men should keep out of feminist criticism.

iii

Men who get into arguments with women about feminist criticism are often given the impression that they are disqualified from doing so simply because they are men. I find the objection puzzling, given the fact that feminists have put a great deal of effort into explaining the differences between sex and gender, the former being a biological category, and the latter (in Sally McConnell-Ginet's neat definition) 'the cultural meaning attached to sexual identity'.[7] The purpose of making this distinction has been to free women (but inevitably men too) from sexist stereotyping based on limiting conceptions of their 'nature'; and the upshot has been a discrediting of essentialistic theories of human behaviour which designate certain characteristics as male-specific and others as female-specific. Consequently, the sense of 'being a woman' cannot be treated as if it were a pre-constructed given – and therefore a source of incontestable authority to be appealed to when the going gets rough in arguments with men – because (like the sense of 'being a man') it is merely the product of sex-coding processes of acculturation. So to hear a woman say that a true understanding of feminist criticism calls for an inwardness beyond the reach of any man sounds like a regression to the bad old days when women had intuition and men had to make do with brains.

There are in fact many ways of discrediting men who elect to comment on matters of concern to women, ranging from vulgar put-downs ('What would a bloody man know about it?') to high-falutin psychoanalytic talk about the impropriety of thrusting the discourse of the Father into places where it is not welcome. The real cause of concern is that men might react negatively to feminist criticism, thus making the 'natural' progression from suspect males to enemies of the movement. Yet it seems to me that whatever else feminism might be, and whatever ends it might think of itself as serving, by the time it enters literary studies as critical discourse it is just one more way of talking about books. As such it must undergo the kind of inspection made sooner or later of every type of critical discourse, each of which has its own aetiology and aims, distinctive features and operational procedures, all of which can be described and assessed for the insights they yield. Now this is not the attitude commonly taken by men who move into the feminist domain and are fortunate enough to be tolerated there. Why they should want to get involved in such a trouble-spot is of course puzzling to many people, men as well as women. Most men who write feminist criticism are professed radicals with a passion for oppositional discourse, and who see radical feminism as a moment of exemplary resistance to an oppressive regime. Personal relationships with feminist women aside, their attitude to feminism is one of commitment rather than curiosity, and they take it up not for something to do but as something that needs to be done. They maintain their credibility by contributing ideological expertise and rhetorical skills towards the construction of a feminist critique which will not be vulnerable to attacks by antifeminists or the corrosions of scepticism. Their response to the challenge of feminism is admirable, for by taking a supportive role in its activities they are doing something positive by way of compensation for the scandal of left-wing male indifference to the women's movement in the sixties.

Nevertheless, I object to a strategy which situates men in such a way that the only speaking positions available to them are those of tame feminist or wild antifeminist. Neither accommodates my own experience as a reader of feminist criticism, which, put briefly, is that the theory is more impressive than some of the practices. For if you are persuaded by what I take to be the central hypothesis of feminist literary criticism – that gender is a crucial determinant in the production, circulation and consumption of literary discourses – and if in addition you feel (as I do) that some of the evidence adduced in support of that hypothesis looks rigged, then inevitably you will find yourself wanting to occupy that discursive space already mapped out by Janet Radcliffe Richards in *The sceptical feminist* (Harmondsworth, 1980). The gist of that book is that a much better case can be made out for feminism than many feminists have succeeded in making. And the corollary of this is that just as language is too important a phenomenon to be turned over entirely to certain types of linguist, so the female 'problematic' (the questions asked of the evidence) is too important to be left in the hands of anti-intellectual feminists, whether vulgarians ('Now don't try to reason with *me*') or highbrows who believe that the construction of logical arguments and verification procedures for handling evidence can be dispensed with, on the grounds that such things are coded as masculine in our society and are therefore quite irrelevant to the discussion and analysis of purely female 'experience'.

The exclusionist view that feminist criticism is essentially women's work and should remain so originates in a separatist conception of the subject wholly at odds with the conditions in which feminist discourses circulate. For even when written by and purportedly for women, feminist literary criticism is read also by men who make a living from talking about books. No teacher of literary studies can afford to ignore feminist contributions to marxist-based critiques of the institutionalisation of literature, particularly the indictment of androcentricity as manifested by the preponderance of male authors on academic syllabuses. Indeed, any man who wanted to ignore it would find it difficult to do so, since feminist criticism turns up in many places other than feminist journals, and feminist presses are not the only ones to publish feminist books. If he is resolute in his machismo, none of it will have much effect on him, although he may find himself becoming more circumspect in what he says about women writers and women critics, unless he is the sort of man who takes pleasure in parading himself as the last unregenerate sexist in a world of wimps. For many men, however, the feminist critique of gender is intellectually disturbing (how could men have been so blind?) and a source of shame and guilt (after such knowledge, what forgiveness?). Even in its milder forms, feminist discourse strikes men as being accusatory, as it is meant to do; and in its most uncompromising manifestations it is unrelentingly intimidatory.

Feminist terrorism is a mirror image of machismo. Unregenerately separatist – men are the problem, so how could they possibly be part of the solution? – it offers the vicarious satisfactions of retaliation and reprisal in a war of the sexes for which the only acceptable end is unconditional surrender of all power to women. Terrorism polarises the sexes in such a way that men must either ignore feminism or attack it, thus 'proving' by such negative actions that women have nothing to gain from listening to moderates and gradualists who believe that inequality is not an eternal and immutable consequence of relations between the sexes, but rather the product of a particular construction of those relations which can and must be remodelled in such a way that neither sex will feel dominated by the other. By contrast with terrorism, therefore, the *j'accuserie* of moderatism is at least negotiable, although even here the options for a man are still limited, unless he is willing to reconstruct himself as a convert and offer to expiate his guilt by becoming that singular anomaly, the male feminist or (to use a less contentious term) pro-feminist male. Nevertheless, it is still said that sympathetic men who understand what feminism is about will have the sense to let women get on with it by themselves; that because men are accustomed to running things, they would take over feminism if given half the chance, their appropriation of it thus constituting yet another form of oppression − 'giving' women what is theirs by right; that men who display no wish to appropriate feminism may well be motivated by an unconscious desire to subvert it; and that academic men who profess to take an 'interest' in feminism (and turn out to have similar 'interests' in marxism, psychoanalysis and so forth) will blunt the cutting edge of its radicalism by academicising it, converting it into an optional 'approach' to literature and offering it as something at once novel and 'relevant' to students bored with traditional approaches.

These arguments can be mounted more persuasively than my crude summary of them might suggest, but all of them are weakened by the fact that even this most recent of feminisms is heavily dependent on men to articulate its position, and continues to co-opt their services. In matters of theory, John Stuart Mill's *The subjection of women* (1869) and Friedrich Engels' *The origin of the family, private property and the state* (1884) are still treated as classic texts, and current feminist criticism would be inconceivable without Michel Foucault's work on discursive formations, the semiology of Roland Barthes, the deconstruction of Jacques Derrida, and Jacques Lacan's imbrication of psychoanalysis with linguistics. In addition to these major contributions by male theorists towards the mobilising of feminist criticism, there is the exemplary feminism of various male writers who succeeded in not being prisoners of their sex. These include Samuel Richardson, a radical feminist in comparison with a male chauvinist like Henry Fielding, and whose *Clarissa* is now being presented to us as 'arguably the major feminist text of the language';[8] Henrik Ibsen, who in such plays as *A doll's house* (1879) and *Hedda Gabler* (1890) embodies the frustrations and tragedy of women trapped in the conventions of a patriarchal society; George Bernard Shaw, who thought a man was simply a woman without petticoats,[9] believed himself to be as good a feminist as Mary Wollstonecraft, and wrote *The quintessence of Ibsenism* in an attempt to prove it; George Meredith, who takes apart in *The egoist* that syndrome later to be called male chauvinism; Henry James, whose novel *The Bostonians* strikes even a 'resisting' reader like Judith Fetterley as an almost faultless analysis of the power struggles between men and women as social classes;[10] Thomas Hardy, who challenged the sexual ideology of his time in creating characters like Tess Durbeyfield and Sue Bridehead, whose failure to conform to acceptable patterns of behaviour caused social upheavals which are replicated in formal disruptions in the novels.

All this work proves that long before the distinction was clearly drawn between a biologically given sex and a socially constructed gender, it was possible for certain male writers to reconstruct themselves temporarily as women for the purposes of creating female characters so untrammelled by contemporary conventional representations of womanhood that women readers even nowadays are amazed that men should have had such insights into what it means to live as a woman in a male-dominated society. Nevertheless, the knowledge that some of the best feminist writing in print has been done by men arouses resentment among those whose mission is to put women on top. Susan Hardy Aiken finds it necessary, for instance, to defend John Stuart Mill against those who would see him as being 'implicated in the very conventions he attacks' in *The subjection of women*, and who would interpret his defence of women as a chivalric gesture 'masking an essential contempt' for women who are thus presumed incapable of defending themselves.[11] Poor Mill; like all men, he is placed in a no-win situation by this type of discourse, for if he had ignored the servitude of Victorian women he would have been callous, and seeing that he doesn't he is patronising. Had he not written so well and so influentially this problem would never have arisen. As it is, the calibre of Mill's book is an embarrassment to the Women Only school of feminist criticism, and their adverse response to it constitutes a cynical warning to any man who tries his hand at feminist criticism: if you have to do it, make sure you don't do it better than women.

So the pertinent question is not whether men are capable of writing about feminism, for clearly they are, but whether or not they should be encouraged. (They can hardly be prevented from doing so, I might add, except by gatekeepers of the feminist publishing network, who might be tempted to indulge in retaliatory exclusionism on behalf of all those women whose writings never got into print because men stood in the way.) The separatist answer to this question is that men should be discouraged from writing feminist literary criticism for the same reason that they should be discouraged from teaching in women's studies courses, namely (as Robin Rowland puts it) that 'having the oppressor lecture on his oppression to the oppressed' is morally suspect.[12] This is to assume, however, that the identification of men with oppression is not an idea to be examined (are women never oppressed by women?) but an unquestionable article of faith.

A more moderate position would seek to erode separatism in the interests of integration on the far side of enlightenment, and encourage men not so much to write feminist criticism *per se* as to incorporate the lessons of feminism into everything they write. In this way they would contribute towards that transformation of society which will render superfluous a good deal of current feminist polemic. Literary criticism has little to gain from a separatist feminism which ghettoes itself as a subculture and risks solipsism by closing off communication with that half of the human race which is the source of its troubles. From the point of view of those in the academies, however, its principal deficiency is that it constitutes itself as a faith to be fortified rather than as a truth-claim to be investigated. This is one of the reasons why it is difficult for a male academic to criticise feminist criticism. Indeed, it is difficult for the academies themselves to accommodate feminism as a faith, as they are much more experienced in training people to 'know' than to 'be', and tend to employ teachers to impart knowledge rather than gurus to implant 'wisdom'. The academies are better equipped, in other words, to teach feminism as a subject than to breed feminists. This is not to deny that many students will indeed become feminists after learning about feminism, just as many become marxists after learning about marxism; but they do so, as it were, in their own time. You may or may not become more patriotic as a result of studying in an institute of learning the history of your own country, but you will be assessed academically on your knowledge of that history, not on your patriotism or lack of it. This could be considered an argument for redefining education in such a way that 'knowing' would be de-privileged and made subservient to 'being', in which case the academies could start producing patriots or feminists or whatever in the way that seminaries turn out priests. But in the meantime, unless the consequence of separatist feminism is to be separatist academics, feminism as a faith can hardly thrive (except in a ghettoed condition) in the academies as at present constituted, with their networks of prerequisite and corequisite subjects, in-term assessment and end-of-year examinations, and all the paraphernalia which maintain that state-supported apparatus of hierarchical grading and accreditation which western societies regard as indispensable to the preservation and dissemination of knowledge.

Feminism is something which everybody should know about, and what better place to encourage such enquiries than the academies, skilled as they are in methods of historical investigation and critical analysis? To claim that feminism would be damaged if treated in this way is ill advised, not only because such an attitude smacks of the worst kind of Romantic anti-intellectualism ('We murder to dissect'), but also because protectionism damages feminism by encouraging the suspicion that anything not available for inspection in the usual ways must have something wrong with it. If feminist criticism is to be a contribution to knowledge, those who write it must expect to receive adverse criticism from men as well as women, and to modify their work accordingly if persuaded that their initial hypotheses have been wrong. Many feminists, however, treat adverse criticism not as part of a process towards knowledge but as a threat to an immutable truth which is known already, believing that those who are not with them must be against them. But the only way in which feminist criticism can enter the academies and make its way there is as a new knowledge which entertains its fundamental tenets as hypotheses rather than beliefs, and understands that such hypotheses will receive provisional acceptance only for as long as they are able to withstand attempts to disconfirm them. The radical thrust of feminist literary criticism is the hypothesis that all writing is 'marked' by gender, and that non-feminist criticism is flawed because it fails to take account of this phenomenon. Such a claim can be validated not by treating it as a revelation for which supporting evidence must be found at all costs but by trying to discover whether or not it is true. And that involves facing up to the possibility that some of the 'evidence' presented in support of it ought not to be dignified with that name at all. There is nothing to stop women from doing the work of disconfirmation entirely on their own, of course, as Maria Black and Rosalind Coward do in their devastating review of *Man made language*.[13] But in some respects it is easier for men than for women to object to the more ridiculous manifestations of feminist criticism, simply because the intimidatory rhetoric of radical feminism designates any woman who is sharply critical of feminist discourse as a female equivalent of the 'white-arsed nigger' of separatist black rhetoric. So whereas a man might feel he has nothing to lose in expressing contempt for the protectionism manifest, for example, in Dale Spender's decision not to engage in adverse criticism of the women discussed in *Women of ideas* — because to do so would be to give men even more ammunition to use against women[14] — a woman might feel diffident about having herself represented as a patriarchally brain-washed traitor to her own sex simply for saying that women don't always see eye to eye with one another, and can even be wrong about some things.

The writing of feminist literary criticism by men is likely to go on being a controversial activity, if only because within that bundle of discursive practices which get labelled feminist there is no agreement as to whether men should be tolerated at all, or what they might be permitted to do if they were. None of this has very much bearing on the kind of activity I am engaging in here, which is to look at feminist criticism as some sort of criticism rather than as some sort of doctrine. For it seems to me that objections raised against the involvement of men in the creation of a feminist literature not only weaken at the discursive level of feminist literary criticism, but disappear altogether at the metacritical level, where the object of enquiry is the validity of critical strategies rather than the truth or falsehood of the ideologies which those strategies articulate. It is no more necessary to be a woman in order to analyse feminist criticism as criticism than it is to be a marxist in order to comprehend the strategies of marxist criticism. In any case, whether or not men are eligible to take part in feminist literary studies at any level is an argument created and sustained solely within the domain of feminist discourse. It cannot possibly be regarded therefore as a prediscursive or extradiscursive mandate for the production and control of feminist criticism.

iv

Feminist literary criticism is at present a congeries of diverse practices, each of which is based on some idea − acknowledged or otherwise − of how a feminist who happens to be working in English studies might best spend her time there. (There is of course a pragmatic brand of feminism which holds that more urgent tasks face feminists than the investigation of English literature, and that time devoted to researching yet another article on yet another woman writer could be spent much more profitably in political activism in that 'real' world where real women have real problems, and in fronting up to the harrowing situations to be encountered in women's shelters and rape crisis centres. But that kind of feminism lies outside the scope of the present enquiry, which is concerned only with the writings of feminists who agree that language and literature are worth studying for feminist purposes − 'reading a novel can be a political activity'[15] − but differ on the question of how to go about it.)

A comprehensive book on the discrimination of feminisms would give not only a diachronic account of those literary movements which have been labelled 'feminist' in the past but also a synchronic account of different practices which constitute 'our' feminism, that is, the one which got under way in the late 1960s and presented its most provocative challenge to English studies in 1970 with the publication of Kate Millett's *Sexual politics*. The value of a diachronic enquiry is to remind us that 'our' feminism is merely the most recent of a number of earlier ones, many of them focused on a key text, such as Virginia Woolf's *A room of one's own* (1929), John Stuart Mill's *The subjection of women* (1869), Mary Wollstonecraft's *A vindication of the rights of woman* (1792), or Mary Astell's *A serious proposal to the ladies for the advancement of their true and greatest interest* (1694). If we were to trawl outside British waters, the diachronic haul would include many other texts going back as far as Aristophanes' comedy *Lysistrata*, which is about how women achieved social change by withholding sexual favours from their men. It would also include phenomena like that *querelle des femmes* instigated by Christine de Pisan with her *Epistre au dieu d'amours* (1399), which was written against the misogynistic representation of women in Jean de Meun's *Roman de la rose*, and which Jean E. Perkins has described as the first overtly feminist criticism of a major literary work.[16]

Each of these can be thought of as constituting a significant 'moment' in a history of feminist criticism which could turn out to be more difficult to write than might be supposed. The principal reason for this is that you have to decide what narrative structure to impose on what looks rather like an intermittent series of discrete feminisms stretching over several centuries: is it a record of continuity or of discontinuity? If you think it politic to argue that current feminism is not just a mad-cap idea dreamed up in the mad-cap 1960s, but a resurgence of important interests with a venerable tradition, then you will be tempted to stress continuities in order to argue that there has always been a feminism. But in doing so you will encounter difficulties caused by the fact that the values and concerns of 'our' feminism may not coincide exactly with those of earlier ones. There are two ways of circumventing this problem, neither of which is wholly satisfactory. One is to 'modernise' earlier feminisms by means of anachronistic readings which are produced by retrojecting current preoccupations on to texts which up till recently were thought innocent of them. This is done by arguing, for example, that problems experienced as emotional by female characters in a novel by Charlotte Brontë – and which earlier readers, at the novelist's own prompting, were inclined to treat as psychological – are 'really' political problems created by a patriarchal system which is especially hard on women who refuse to conform to patriarchally acceptable roles. Hence Rosemary Dinnage's objection that Gilbert and Gubar's *The madwoman in the attic* (1979) tends to see nineteenth-century women writers in terms of late twentieth-century feminism, making them new by making them relevant to current ways of thinking about women, but not differentiating sufficiently between the way we are now and the way they were then.[17] The other tactic available to historians of continuity who wish to avoid constructing earlier feminisms on our terms is to operate with a 'weak' (or generalised) definition of feminism, such that vague similarities to a current concern can be construed as prefigurative instances of it, promulgated by people who are then given the status of 'forerunners' or proto-feminists. The attraction of a 'weak' definition is that it evades a couple of problems which are connected with the formulation of 'strong' or stipulative definitions: first, deciding which characteristics of feminism – whether 'ours' or someone else's – are to be considered normative, and secondly, applying the resulting definition in a non-prescriptive manner. But the drawbacks of working with a weak definition are nicely described by Janet Todd in response to recent recuperations of eighteenth-century feminism:

If 'feminism', in a 1970s sense, claims absolute equality of the sexes and complex identification of roles, then no woman in eighteenth-century England advocated it; if it implies equal opportunity, then probably only Mary Wollstonecraft, who hinted at female politicians while extolling motherhood, might qualify. But if a feminist is one who is aware of female problems and is angry or mildly irritated at the female predicament, then almost every woman writer and many men could claim the title.[18]

Given what appears to be Hobson's choice between 'strong' readings of earlier feminisms, which spuriously modernise them, and 'weak' readings, which are insufficiently discriminating, the historian of feminist criticism might well opt for discontinuity as a less troublesome model.

To do so would be to proceed on the assumption that because diachronic feminisms are sometimes separated from one another by hundreds of years and emerge in different conditions they can never be identical, and therefore the relation between one and another is marked more distinctively by differences than similarities. A reading of *Clarissa* which emphasises similarities will produce Samuel Richardson as a radical feminist whose decision to ground fiction in the exploration of female consciousness makes his novel 'readable' for those twentieth-century women who placed consciousness-raising on their initial programme of activities. ('Readable', in such contexts, signifies 'politically relevant', rather than what bookish people mean by 'a good read': *Clarissa* has always been a good read for people who like to lose themselves in big novels, but only in the context of recent feminism have its concerns — female sexuality and the inscription of it in cultural practices, including the writing of fiction — become relevantly 'readable'.) An account of the same novel which emphasises differences, on the other hand, will point out that anybody who believes the sorts of things which Richardson believed (such as that chastity is the indispensable condition of female self-sufficiency, and that the patriarchal family should remain the nuclear unit of a stable society) can hardly be called a radical feminist in current senses of the word.[19] Such a reading is likely to support a historicist view of the past, finding most significance in the 'otherness' or alterity of one feminism with respect to another, and warning us that such similarities as we discern between them are either incidental or hallucinatory. 'Continuity' is deemed an illusion created by the contiguity of selected items: we lift things out of their original contexts, talk about them as if they were instances of the same thing, put them into chronological order, and then pretend that the sequence we have thus created constitutes a 'tradition'. In fact, a less selective use of the data might show that feminisms, like many other human phenomena, come and go, and that each not only differs from the others but is also discontinuous with them. Modelling a history of feminist literary criticism is therefore a delicate issue, for if earlier ones have either been suppressed or have just petered out (and therefore compelled the inventors of each new one to start from scratch), then this most recent one may be no exception to the rule. The scholarly desire to discriminate historically between one feminism and another may well conflict, therefore, with the polemical desire to run them together as evidence of a long-standing tradition whose cumulative force is now irrepressible. But I think it a weak position to argue for continuities in spite of evidence to the contrary, and to try to show that current feminism is shored up by all the others. A much stronger position is to concede the randomness and hiatuses of the historical record, but assuage fears about the future of 'our' feminism (whose 'death' keeps being proclaimed with the monotonous regularity reserved a few years ago for the 'death of the novel') by demonstrating that it is more sophisticated theoretically than any of the others have been, and so much better organised that never again will women feel — as this most recent generation of feminists felt — that there is nowhere to begin except at the very beginning.

The diversity revealed by a diachronic survey of feminisms would be shown also in a synchronic account of the different activities which constitute current feminism, each of which is capable of generating a different programme for English studies. There are sociofeminists whose interest in the roles assigned to women in our society prompt studies of the ways in which women are represented in literary texts ('images of women'); there are semiofeminists whose point of departure is semiotics, the science of signs, and who study the signifying practices by means of which females are coded and classified as women in order to be assigned their social roles; there are psychofeminists who forage in Freud and Lacan for a theory of feminine sexuality unconstrained by male norms and categories, and who examine literary texts for unconscious articulations of feminine desire or traces of where it has been repressed; there are marxist feminists more interested in oppression than repression, and who process literary texts in a recognisably marxist manner, infiltrating 'woman' into their discourse at precisely those points where in a non-feminist marxist analysis you would expect to encounter 'the working class'; and there are socio-semio-psycho-marxist feminists who do a little bit of everything as the occasion arises. There are lesbian feminists who promulgate a somatic theory of writing, exploring the connection between sexuality and textuality by looking to the labia as the source of a distinctively feminine writing (*écriture féminine*), thus countering that dominantly phallocentric myth of writing as an erectile and ejaculatory activity. And there are black feminists, who feel themselves to be doubly if not triply oppressed: as blacks in a white supremacist society, as women in a patriarchy, and as workers under capitalism. Their indictment of recent feminism for concentrating almost exclusively on the problems of middle-class white women in technologically advanced societies is set out memorably in the writings of Angela Davis, and forms the hinterland to the resentment expressed by Gloria T. Hull who, finding herself the token black contributor to a collection of feminist literary essays called *Shakespeare's sisters* (1979), began by saying, 'Black women poets are not "Shakespeare's sisters".'[20]

Such is the range of practices tolerated that there is even room for feminists who object to being called 'feminist', and who believe that the term 'feminism' has lost whatever revolutionary potential it once had, because feminism is so compromised by patriarchy's accommodation of it as to be styled more accurately *phalloféminisme*.[21] 'Feminism', according to the French *Psych et po* group, 'is precisely the reinforcement of the privileged relationship to the Patriarch (seductive, transgressive, identificatory, etc.)';[22] and so the Parisian feminists-who-are-not-'feminists' — the 'anti-feminist' feminists — pursue the idea of the feminine (*le féminin*) not as something related specifically to women but as the signifier of a force which has always been excluded from the patriarchal order of things, and which is capable therefore of disrupting that order to the point of destroying it. This diversity of aims and practices enables current feminism to advance on several fronts at once, which is generally thought of as a strength which would be lacking in a monolithic feminism. The shifting of boundaries between one type of activity and another is seen as evidence of growth and transformation, which are healthy signs in what is after all a 'movement' and not a fixity. Consequently, attempts to define feminist writing are looked upon with suspicion on the grounds that definitions are bound to be premature at this stage and perhaps oppressively prescriptive. 'It is impossible to *define* a feminist practice of writing', Hélène Cixous warns, 'and this is an impossibility that will remain, for this practice can never be theorized, enclosed, coded — which doesn't mean that it doesn't exist.'[23] But we all have a rough idea of what feminist writing is like, even if we cannot define it exactly. And the same is true of feminist criticism. Cixous' dismissal of definition as an impossibility in the case of women's writing masquerades as a warning to the foolhardy but is clearly protectionist towards a feminism which, fearing foreclosure of its activities, wisely promotes openness and plurality as its distinguishing features, but grounds itself vulnerably on the theory that it cannot be theorised. A working definition of feminist literary criticism does not strike me as being either impossible or undesirable.

One striking feature of feminist metacriticism has been its attempt to describe the different types of feminist criticism not as equally available options but as constituting an evolutionary sequence. By the time 'our' feminism was only ten years old it was already spoken of as being in its third phase, having gone through 'early' attacks on the sexism of books written by male chauvinists (androtexts), concentrated 'later' on the specificity of women's writing (gynotexts), and arrived subsequently at the phase we are in now, which is characterised by a pervasive interest in theory, much of it provoked allegedly by difficulties encountered in the first two phases of this brief history.[24] This supersessional model of feminist criticism implies that feminism has progressed in a linear fashion, driven (like everything else) by the demon of progress from early crudities to later sophistications. Yet to browse through current feminist journals − the cheaply produced ones as well as those which are as impeccably turned out as *Signs* − is to realise that this is very much a third-phase view of feminist literary criticism, and that many women who think of themselves as in some way feminist still engage energetically in first-phase exposés of androtexts as well as in second-phase explorations of gynotexts. Clearly, feminism has an avant-garde which is more alert to the theoretical implications of what it means to 'do' feminist criticism than the general regiment of women, some of whose activities it finds correspondingly embarrassing. The regiment writes in English about books written in English. Its criticism is usually called 'Anglo-American', although it might be designated more properly 'anglophone' in view of the major contributions made by feminists who are neither English nor American. Beyond this anglophone sphere is a large and increasingly influential body of francophone writing which is known as 'French feminism' and includes the work of Hélène Cixous, Luce Irigaray and Julia Kristeva. The most convenient introduction to it for anglophone readers is an anthology of translations called *New French feminisms* (1980), a book which is sometimes criticised for having mistaken the most visible work of Parisian feminists for the most representative, and for giving undue emphasis to its most hermetic features.[25] Like a good deal of recent French criticism, French feminism assumes in the reader an advanced knowledge of linguistics, philosophy and psychoanalysis; it assumes also a passion for abstraction, particularly the theorising of theory, which is in marked contrast to the anglophone tradition that the only theories worth bothering about are those which have practical applications to particular texts. Because French feminist criticism is correspondingly difficult to read for people not educated in the French tradition, the presentation of it to anglophone feminists has been accompanied by exactly the same blend of mystification and snobbery which characterised attempts to introduce structuralism into non-feminist anglophone criticism. Francophile feminists often adopt a patronisingly more-Parisian-than-thou attitude towards their anglophone sisters, who are seen as muddling along in conditions of benighted empiricism instead of getting themselves an adequate theory of the text.

Consequently, in francophile circles, 'Anglo-American' is a derogatory term with some of the connotations which 'liberal humanist' has acquired in marxist literary criticism.

Seeing that so many of the preoccupations of current feminism are latent already in *A room of one's own* (1929), it might seem remarkable that Woolf's book had no impact whatsoever on mainstream literary criticism in the 1930s; but it is even more remarkable that the upheavals created by Millett's *Sexual politics* in the 1970s should not have been created twenty years earlier by Simone de Beauvoir's formidable indictment of patriarchal injustice to women, *The second sex*, (1949), an abridged English version of which was published in 1953. Various explanations have been put forward of why Millett's book seemed to come at the right time. Here, for example, is Catharine R. Stimpson's list of factors which prepared the way for 1970s feminism:

the entrance of women, of all classes and races, into the public labor force and political processes; a partial secularization of society, which softened the power of traditional religions in the formation of identity and institutions; a greater belief in supplementary ideologies that praised equality and autonomy; and a democratization of education and culture that permitted women to participate in them more freely.[26]

We can all think of ways in which such a list might be supplemented, ranging from the highly organised lobbying of policy makers on behalf of women's rights to the availability of the contraceptive pill which, by enabling women to control their own reproductive processes, must have contributed at least as much to their independence, both literally and symbolically, as any theorising of their personal autonomy. For many, a crucial factor in the mobilising of contemporary feminism was the large number of educated and articulate women who were politically radicalised in the 1960s by the Vietnam war, and who learned from marxist writings the importance of theory for revolutionary action – so much so as to be able to capitalise on their disaffection from the residual sexism of left-wing men by constructing an ideology of their own, a feminist ideology, along marxist lines. In the academies, feminist critics could ally themselves with marxist critics in attacks on the class-bound elitism of traditional literature syllabuses, and on the political inadequacies of 'aesthetic' criticism; and lessons could be learned from the recent successes and failures of black studies in how to organise a new type of critical discourse around a new literary object. The subsequent weakening of faith in traditional literary studies – culminating most recently in the so-called 'crisis' in English studies –

has provided unprecedented opportunities for shifting feminism from the margins to the centre of a redefined conception of what is involved in the study of literature. But in order to bring off that manoeuvre you first need to have a comprehensive and comprehensible theory of feminist criticism, the lineaments of which we should now consider.

2

Constructing feminist theories of criticism

Every critical method is a scanning device for picking up particular types of information, which it logs by means of a technical vocabulary specially invented for this purpose. The point of inventing a new device is to reveal what was previously invisible, and in that way to articulate a new kind of knowledge. An X-ray photograph is totally different from a snapshot of the same object, and different again from an ultraviolet photograph. All three photographs represent different kinds of knowledge, and each is produced by a different method. Feminist criticism is a scanning device in this sense: it operates in the service of a new knowledge which is constructed by rendering visible the hitherto invisible component of 'gender' in all discourses produced by the humanities and the social sciences. As such, it rivals the two major new knowledges which have challenged the autonomy of literary studies since the 1930s, marxism and psychoanalysis, which focus respectively on the material and unconscious conditions in which cultural artefacts are first produced and then reproduced in critical discourse.

Literary studies is one of many things which new knowledges such as these have to account for, and they do so by first exposing its hidden presuppositions and then giving it a different objective. This involves opposing the commonsense view that the only way to study literature is to read lots of it, and substituting instead the proposition that literature is best studied as a manifestation of shaping forces which are fundamental to the kind of society we have inherited, and which will have to be altered if we want a better one. It then becomes feasible to propose the dismantlement of traditional literary studies as a self-justifying activity in a restricted field, and to redefine literature as symptomatic of those concerns which the new knowledge has deemed centrally important through its axial hypothesis. As a result, literature may well lose some of the specificity it is credited with in aesthetic or formalistic modes of enquiry. Yet at the same time, new knowledges offer to rescue literary studies from its self-imposed isolation from the rest of society and to situate it in the mainstream of cultural enquiry, provided it is willing to treat literature as symptomatic of tendencies discernible in other cultural practices, some of which are less exalted and have correspondingly less kudos attached to the study of them. The controversy which goes on whenever a new knowledge makes a bid for literary studies is mainly about whether the alleged gains will outweigh the feared losses should a take-over occur.

People involved in consolidating a new knowledge usually put a great deal of effort into designing and refining those discovery procedures which collectively constitute its method, and which later generations inherit as 'methodological' problems. A striking feature of some American feminist criticism, therefore, is its decision to declare its field resistant to the development of a coherent theory. 'In order to write a new history worthy of the name', says Gerda Lerner, 'we will have to recognize that no single methodology and conceptual framework can fit the complexities of the historical experience of all women.'[1] That is the moderate form of the argument: a dispersed field demands diverse methods, and methodological tidiness leads to reductionism and oversimplification. The more radical claim, made, for instance, by Annis V. Pratt, is that 'methodolatry' is something which feminists can very well do without, because 'the insistence upon a single method is not only disfunctional but an attribute of the patriarchy'; and therefore Mary Daly advocates 'Methodicide' on the grounds that 'the Methodolatry of patriarchal disciplines kills creative thought'.[2] Unlike psychoanalysis and marxism, of course, feminism does not have the equivalent of a founding 'father' – nor could it have, seeing that that in itself is a patriarchal notion of how knowledge is created and authorised. It is considerably easier, therefore, for feminists to disavow theory than it would be for a marxist or a psychoanalytic critic, each of whom inherits a complex body of methodological procedures. But anti-theoreticism is a dangerous position to adopt, as Mary Evans points out, for it threatens to restrict feminism to a 'primitive subjectivism' which is 'characteristic of some of the most reactionary social organizations in existence'.[3]

Disavowals of theory and method are likely to cause more problems for feminists in the social sciences than for those involved in English studies, which until recently was not in the habit of worrying about things like that. A classic statement of the methodless methodism of English studies is the exchange between René Wellek and F. R. Leavis in the March and June 1937 issues of *Scrutiny*: Leavis refused to concede that his influential encounters with a great variety of texts could be systematised in terms of a theory, despite the fact that his imitators had no difficulty at all in abstracting a method from the master's performances and turning out 'Leavisite' criticism. Structuralists attempted to bring to literary studies something of the methodological rigour aimed at in that descriptive linguistics on which their activities were based. But when the most versatile of the structuralist critics, Roland Barthes, started writing post-structuralist criticism, method was found once again to be 'ultimately sterile' and therefore something which critics must either 'turn against' or regard as being 'without any founding privilege'.[4] The Barthesian recantation came as no surprise to those who had felt all along that Barthes was not really a method-man at all, but simply presented his insights in such a way as to create the illusion of method. Suddenly, principled opportunism was back in fashion as a critical strategy, and in a world which had fetishised theory to an unprecedented degree Iain McGilchrist launched his polemic *Against criticism* (London, 1982), in which the only method advocated is that which is 'the denial of all pre-existing methods' – his reason being that 'the only genuine critical theory is that of no-theory' (pp. 13–14). This is a bold response to the left-wing charge that critics who claim not to have a theory are merely in the grip of an unacknowledged one. My purpose in drawing attention to such developments, however, is to point out that objections to making feminist criticism part of English studies are not based on its eclecticism or its indifference to methodological rigour, each of which is likely to be regarded as an asset rather than a liability.

Feminist criticism draws on a number of discursive strategies – marxist, structuralist, and post-structuralist or deconstructionist – which developed in opposition to what is called 'practical criticism' in Britain and 'new criticism' in North America. Let us begin with the relationship between feminism and marxism.

ii

'Radical feminism,' notes Carol McMillan, with an eye for a provocative analogy, 'grew from a spare rib of leftist revolutionary politics.'[5] Its birthplace was America in the 1960s, where one of the problems faced by an educated new left was a familiar one for marxist intellectuals: to sustain interest in revolutionary action among the poor whites and poorer blacks who constitute the working classes. Most working-class people would much rather become middle class than classless, and quickly lose whatever interest they might be persuaded to take in revolutionary proposals for the redistribution of wealth in society once they themselves become more affluent in their own eyes and see prospects of upward mobility for their children. Fortunately, the revolutionary ardour of those disaffected young men and women who formed the student protest groups which constituted the new left could be channelled into other and equally worthwhile objectives, notably opposition to racism through the civil rights movement, and to imperialism through the peace movement which sought to terminate the increasingly futile military involvement of 'Amerika' in Vietnam.

Women who joined the protest movements soon discovered, however, that the egalitarianism and altruism which motivated such interventions in race relations and international affairs were not thought of by new left men as relevant to their personal relations with new left women, who were expected to perform (in a quite unrevolutionary manner) domestic and sexual services for the men who saw themselves as the decision makers. At a 1964 meeting of the SNCC, the Student Non-violent Coordinating Committee which was formed to end racial segregation in the southern states of America, Ruby Doris Smith Robinson presented a paper on 'The position of women in SNCC', which elicited Stokely Carmichael's notorious response that 'the only position for women in SNCC is prone'.[6] Claims by radical women that they were being exploited by men in the same way that blacks are exploited by whites – and that sexism is no less intolerable than racism – were dismissed disparagingly as 'pussy power' politics or evidence of 'clit militancy', thus provoking spirited counterattacks on 'cock privilege' like the one by Robin Morgan, who exhorted women to say 'goodbye forever' to the 'counterfeit Left, counterleft, male-dominated cracked-glass-mirror reflection of the Amerikan Nightmare'.[7] For Morgan as for all those other women who defected from new left radicalism to become radical feminists, 'women are the real left'. Marge Piercy's novel *Vida* (New York, 1980) evokes the turmoil of those years which Piercy experienced at first hand, for she was one of the organisers of the SDS (Students for a Democratic Society) before she resigned in 1969 as a result of the intransigently sexist attitudes of SDS men towards women in the organisation.

The question posed by this fracturing of the new left along gender lines is this: what does feminism stand to gain from association with marxism as a revolutionary doctrine, seeing that every man in the new left could be presumed to be at least sympathetic to marxism? Marxism identifies capitalism (and the modes of production which support it) as the material base of a class system which is the source of all oppression, and holds that the specific subjection of women will end necessarily in that general demise of oppression which is to follow the destruction of capitalism. 'The subjection of woman' is therefore not a special case with a different aetiology: 'There are no women', says one of the men in Christina Stead's novel *Seven poor men of Sydney* (1934). 'There are only dependent and exploited classes, of which women make one.'[8] Many women disagree. 'We do not believe', wrote the New York Radical Feminists in 1969, 'that capitalism, or any .other economic system, is the cause of female oppression, nor do we believe that female oppression will disappear as a result of purely economic revolution.'[9] For them it is patriarchy which is the problem, not economics. The rival marxist view is put succinctly, however, by Simone de Beauvoir when she says she 'never cherished any illusion of changing woman's condition' because she believed that that could be achieved 'only at the price of a revolution in production. That is why', she adds, 'I avoided falling into the trap of ''feminism''.'[10] Each of these rival positions seeks to explain why things are as bad as they are for women by positing an original oppression which is economic exploitation in the one case and primal rape in the other. Where you stand on this issue will determine whether you see marxism as the key to social transformation and the liberation of women, or merely as the model for a rival transformational system which regards male domination as the base on which the sexist superstructure of society stands. 'The question', as Sheila Delaney puts it, 'is whether bottom line is the sex line or the class line.'[11]

Women who call themselves marxist–feminists object to having the issue polarised in this way, and prefer to work with a model which allows for what Heidi Hartmann calls 'two separate but interlocking sets of social relations, capitalism and patriarchy, each with a material base, each with its own dynamic'.[12] Consequently, it should not be a matter of privileging class over gender or vice versa, but of engaging in the much more difficult task of showing how and where such 'interlockings' occur, which is what the London based Marxist–Feminist Literature Collective set out to do in its readings of three novels by Charlotte Brontë.[13] As the interpretation of *Shirley* reveals, however, it is much easier to produce feminist alternatives to marxist readings than marxist–feminist interlockings. Helen Taylor, for example, ends up rejecting the marxist view (proposed by Terry Eagleton) that Chartism is 'the unspoken subject' of *Shirley*, and sets in its place the feminist view that 'the fully spoken political subject of the novel is the urgent plight of dependent women'.[14] A more coherent marxist–feminist reading, on the other hand, would interlock a spoken feminism with an unspoken Chartism and see them both as constitutive elements of the social formation in which *Shirley* first appeared.

Marx himself had relatively little to say about the oppression of women, a subject he appears to have deputed to Friedrich Engels. In *The origin of the family* (1884) Engels bypasses the problem of primacy by arguing that 'the first class oppression coincides with that of the female sex by the male', thus legitimating the familiar equation of husbands with the bourgeoisie and wives with the proletariat.[15] Any social system in which a marxist analysis uncovers oppressive practices becomes metaphorical in feminist rhetoric of the oppression of women: class, race, slavery and colonisation furnish the dominant tropes of oppression. If male–female relations are construed in class terms, for instance, men are always the ruling class: for as August Strindberg explains in his preface to *Miss Julie* (written in 1888), the aristocratic Julie is sexually 'mastered' by her father's servant 'simply because he is a man. Sexually he is an aristocrat.'[16] If the trope shifts from class to caste, women become hopeless and helpless untouchables: 'one can leave one class in order to move into another', notes Simone de Beauvoir, 'but caste is the group into which one is born and which one cannot leave'.[17] If white women are imagined to be metaphorical blacks, then the scandalous 'invisibility' of black people in a white society – a subject which receives its best-known literary treatment in Ralph Ellison's novel *Invisible man* (1952) – becomes the model for delineating the corresponding invisibility of women in a patriarchy; and thus the denial of opportunities to women constitutes an apartheid. And because the history of black–white relations is also the history of slavery, the analogy with slavery is present already in Mary Wollstonecraft's *A vindication of the rights of woman* (1792) and becomes the dominant trope in nineteenth-century feminist writing, doubtless because of feminist involvement in the abolitionist movement. 'No slave is a slave to the same lengths, and in so full a sense of the word', wrote John Stuart Mill, 'as a wife is.'[18] Sexism, slavery and racism commingle in Elizabeth Barrett Browning's poem 'The runaway slave at Pilgrim's Point' (1850), which is about the flogging to death of a black slave for murdering the child she bore after being raped by her white owner.[19] More recently the subjection of women has been analogised in Third World terms, either as what Beatrix Campbell calls 'visceral colonialism' ('phallic imperialisms, penile tyrannies, and so on'), or as what Anne Summers (following Barbara Burris) sees as a Fourth World of women colonised by men.[20] In this case, the plight of women as a colonised sex becomes susceptible to Frantz Fanon's analysis of colonialism in *The wretched of the earth* (1961). These tropes of oppression function emotively rather than analytically, and are therefore vulnerable to critiques based on questions they suppress. They tend to be unidirectional and irreversible, which means that whereas feminists might find it helpful to think of marriage as slavery for women, no abolitionist would think of slavery as rather like marriage. Furthermore, there is always the danger that some of these tropes – emanating as they do from First World white women – may trivialise the problems faced by black and Third World peoples, and in that way themselves become inadvertently oppressive.

The principal attraction of marxism for feminists who want a better deal for women is that it shows how to analyse a social system with a view to getting it changed. 'The philosophers have only *interpreted* the world, in various ways', wrote Marx; 'the point is to *change* it.'[21] Shifted into a feminist key by Andrea Dworkin, this then reads: 'we intend to change [the world] so totally that someday the texts of masculinist writers will be anthropological curiosities'.[22] All activities therefore become instrumental to that end, including the study of literature, which is not to be undertaken simply for 'its own sake' in a belletristic or aestheticist manner, but as a means of transforming readers who will then go on to transform the world. So Judith Fetterley does not want us to read her book on American fiction as a piece of academic literary criticism – written, as such things tend to be, partly for the intellectual enlightenment of students and colleagues, and partly in the hope of securing tenure or promotion – but as 'a self-defense survival manual for the woman reader lost in "the masculine wilderness of the American novel" '.[23] The obligatory movement is always from theory to praxis, from contemplation to action. 'I am not terribly interested in whether feminism becomes a respectable part of academic criticism', writes Lillian S. Robinson. 'I am very much concerned that feminist critics become a useful part of the women's movement.'[24]

The first step is to recognise that politics is not the sole preserve of professionals called politicians. On the contrary (in Gottfried Keller's aphorism) 'everything is politics',[25] especially those things which claim or are claimed to be apolitical, like those 'truths' which great literature is said to embody, and which still get labelled 'universal', though less often 'eternal' than used to be the case. 'Politics' in this wider sense means 'power' or rather 'power relations': who does what to whom and in whose interests. And because human relationships are necessarily interpersonal, 'the personal is political', to quote a feminist slogan of the 1960s: relations between the sexes are marked by what Wilhelm Reich called 'sexual politics', a phrase which Kate Millett made famous in 1970 in the title of her book. If everything is politics, you cannot be accused of desecrating literature by introducing politics into the study of it, because the politics are there already. Far from 'introducing' sexual politics into literary study, you are merely refusing to suppress the topic any longer. To read a canonical text in a feminist way is to force that text to reveal its hidden sexual ideology which, in so far as it happens to coincide with that of the predominantly male critics who have written about it, tends not to be mentioned in non-feminist criticism.

'Ideology' is that never fully articulated system of assumptions by which a society operates, and which permeates everything it produces, including of course what is deemed to be literature. The term is used in this sense by Louis Althusser, and was mediated for literary critics by Pierre Macherey before being assimilated into English studies by Terry Eagleton.[26] 'Ideology' is manifest in the ways we represent ourselves (and are represented) to one another; 'sexual ideology' determines, for example, what is deemed to be socially acceptable behaviour for men and women. The function of an ideology is to justify the status quo and to persuade the powerless that their powerlessness is inevitable. Fragments of a dominant ideology are sometimes identified by writers and held up for inspection. This is what Conrad does with the ideology of imperialism in *Heart of darkness* (1902), where European greed for the natural resources of Africa is shown to be displaced by a humanitarian desire to 'civilise' the dark continent – an ideology of enlightenment which represents exploitation as trade, and condones murder as a means of eliminating 'savagery'. But the ideologies which interest marxist and feminist critics most are those a writer is unaware of. These are what Penny Boumelha looks for in her study of Thomas Hardy, defining ideology as 'a complex system of representations by which people are inserted as individual subjects into the social formation'.[27] Like any other ideology, sexist ideology – the ideology of male dominance – operates by repressing what is repressible and displacing what is not, thus producing false resolutions of manifest contradictions in our society. One such contradiction is the gap between the ideal of sexual equality in the work-force and the reality of sexual inequality. The indisputable fact of inequality can be either suppressed by the ideology of 'equal opportunity' inherited from meritocratic theories of education, or displaced by the ideology of domestic fulfilment ('A woman's place is in the home'). The business of a critic, therefore, is to examine a literary work for traces of the ideologies which shape it, whether its author was aware of them or not, and to point to discrepancies between what the work purports to tell and what a careful reading of it shows. In this type of enquiry a good book is one which questions the ideologies it articulates, like *Tess of the d'Urbervilles* or *Jude the obscure*, whose heroines are not constrained by contemporary ideologies of female virtue and bourgeois marriage.

'Contradiction' serves much the same function here as 'unity' does in rival modes of literary criticism which operate with organicist metaphors of aesthetic form and seek to persuade us that great literary works are much more unified than we ever suspected. The difference lies in the uses to which these two crucial concepts are put. In liberal humanist criticism, the concept of unity functions as a bonding material to fill in the gaps which are visible to any but the most casual reader of a text. The aim is to unify its disparate parts and give it the illusion of coherence, because in this type of criticism great works of art are always thought of as unified and coherent: anything which is not cannot be great, and may not even be art. In marxist criticism, on the other hand – and in the feminist criticism which derives from it – the aim is not to package the work more coherently than its author managed to do but to rip it apart, with or without the author's cooperation. 'A successful work', according to Theodor W. Adorno, 'is not one which resolves contradictions in a spurious harmony, but one which expresses the idea of harmony negatively by embodying the contradictions, pure and uncompromised, in its innermost structure.'[28] Works which don't do this are believed to have something to hide, and the function of criticism is to show what that is.

There is no doubt that the newer 'contradictionist' criticism can be at least as illuminating as the older 'unificatory' kind was believed to be, and not only when dealing with books written by men, as Mary

Poovey's comments on *Persuasion* show: 'The fact that Jane Austen's novels contain almost no examples of happy marriages despite their inevitable culmination in a happy marriage summarizes both the price of such symbolic resolution and its attractions.'[29] But the drawback of working with contradictionist modes of discourse is the way they recoil upon the user.

Any method which demonstrates the contradictions of capitalism – contradictions which, we are assured, are bound to bring about its collapse sooner or later, because a house divided against itself cannot stand – can be used to demonstrate equally well the contradictions of marxism. It is impossible, in other words, to appropriate the methods of contradictionist criticism without inheriting at least some of its problems.

What this means is that feminists who draw attention to the contradictions of patriarchy are vulnerable to counterattacks on the contradictions of feminism, which are in any case not difficult to detect. Some of these are relatively trivial, such as the case of the fire-breathing anti-patriarch brought up by 'a feminist father', or the intransigent separatist who acknowledges her Ted ('who stands in contradiction to my entire thesis on men').[30] Heterosexual women who prefer the company of what radical doctrine designates the oppressor; daughters who grow up watching good-natured fathers destroyed by domineering wives – such paradoxes can be thematised for wry amusement, furnishing up-to-date instances of life's little ironies, some of which are chronicled by Jill Tweedie in *Letters from a fainthearted feminist* (London, 1982). But they are undoubtedly symptomatic of the central contradiction in feminist discourses: namely, that they claim to speak for all women, many of whom do not want to be spoken for in that way. The feminist dialectic, then, sets women against women as well as against men. Non-feminist women are styled traitors, Aunt Jemimas, domesticated females, *femmes-alibi*, token women and victims of the queen bee syndrome. They include right-wing campaigners like Phyllis Schlafly and organisations with names like Women Who Want to be Women; their objections to feminism are articulated clearly by Arianna Stassinopoulos in *The female woman* (1973) – which answers Germaine Greer's *The female eunuch* (1970) – and by Midge Decter in *The new chastity and other arguments against women's liberation* (1972); and they include also a few ex-feminists of whom the best known is Betty Friedan, the woman credited with giving birth to 'our' feminism in *The feminine mystique* in 1963 and then trying to stifle it in 1981 with *The second stage*, a book which argues that 'sexual politics has been a red herring, an acting-out of feminist reaction'.[31]

'Successful' non-feminist women are a perennial embarrassment to theorists of patriarchal oppression, whether they are writers like Joyce Carol Oates, critics like Susan Sontag or scholars like Helen Gardner. Particularly irksome are those women who deny having written what feminists take to be feminist books: Christina Stead, for instance, told an interviewer in 1979 that *For love alone* (1945) 'has nothing to do with women's liberation', and Doris Lessing was equally hard in 1971 on readers who had tried to appropriate *The golden notebook* (1962) for feminism.[32] And then there are those important women writers who appear to have passed up the opportunity to be more feminist than they turned out to be, such as George Eliot, who worked with men as intellectually their equal, refused to get caught up in the nineteenth-century 'woman question', told Edith Simcox in 1880 that 'she had never all her life cared very much for women', and is therefore not surprisingly the subject of debate as to whether her novels can be considered feminist.[33] Even writers on the side of the feminist angels have their contradictory features, for as Kate Millett reminds us, the feminist who wrote *A room of one's own* (1929) and *Three guineas* (1938) is also the author of a couple of famous novels which 'glorified two housewives, Mrs. Dalloway and Mrs. Ramsay'.[34]

Women who write books which reinforce stereotypical models of feminine behaviour – though not necessarily as blatantly as Louisa May Alcott does in *Little women* (1868) – are usually thought of as casualties of patriarchal brainwashing who have internalised the myth of female inferiority to such a degree that it results in varying stages of disablement, ranging from diffidence to pathological self-hatred, and manifests itself in an unjustifiable contempt for other women's achievements. So when Louise Bogan admits to being less than enthusiastic at the prospect of editing an anthology of 'female verse' ('the thought of corresponding with a lot of female songbirds made me acutely ill'), her remark is taken as evidence not of critical integrity but of psychocultural conditioning: 'obviously', Gilbert and Gubar conclude, 'Bogan had internalized just those patriarchal interdictions that have historically caused women poets from Finch to Plath anxiety and guilt about attempting the pen'.[35] Obviously? Would it never occur to a woman to find the effusions of female songbirds tedious unless some man put her up to it? After reading some recent anthologies of mediocre-to-bad poems by women I am inclined to think that when Bogan said what she did she was speaking as an experienced critic and not as a patriarchal cripple.

Marxist feminism sees patriarchy as an 'ideology' (in Althusser's sense) experienced in the form of what Antonio Gramsci calls a 'hegemony', which Raymond Williams glosses as 'a lived system of meanings and values'. These are 'constitutive and constituting', he adds: they are 'experienced as practices' and appear to be 'reciprocally confirming': the hegemony 'thus constitutes a sense of reality for most people in the society, a sense of absolute because experienced reality'.[36] The aim of a radical feminism is to break that androcentric hegemony which makes women feel that their own sense of reality is at odds with the 'reality' they are expected to conform to. Feminist criticism must therefore be an oppositional practice based on resistance to the dominant hegemony, and its ideal reader (in so far as such a phantom can be imagined) is Judith Fetterley's 'resisting' reader. For if marxists are right in claiming that no reading is innocent, and that we ought to know which readings we are guilty of, then criticism turns into an accusatory activity based on what Paul Ricoeur calls a 'hermeneutics of suspicion'.[37] So one of the things which is demonstrated by resisting readers is that so-called innocent readings in a patriarchy are likely to be guiltily androcentric. By contrast, feminist readings can be 'gynocentric' − woman-centred − without ever being guiltily so, because they never pretend to be anything else. The aim is to convince men that their criticism is never gender-free and universal: when they think and write they do so as men, and not as representatives of the human species.

Whether in fact literary studies should be chosen as the site on which to establish this and similar claims − rather than cultural or communication studies − is a moot point, seeing that far more people watch television programmes and films than read the books which get taught in literary studies. This too is a problem inherited from marxist criticism, and put bluntly by Terry Eagleton in connection with a book by Fredric Jameson: 'how is a Marxist−structuralist analysis of a minor novel of Balzac to help shake the foundations of capitalism?'[38] How, for that matter, is a feminist analysis of D. H. Lawrence's novels, major as well as minor, to help shake the foundations of patriarchy? The best way of answering this question is to rephrase it negatively: why should the works of writers admired in a patriarchal society and prescribed for study in schools and universities be spared the kind of criticism which feminists are making of all our social institutions, including the institution of literature? For as long as 'literature' lasts, it ought to remain on any feminist agenda for social transformation. Feminist criticism got under way after turning to marxism to learn how to mobilise an oppositional discourse. It has applied what it learnt so well that it is regarded by marxists as an exemplary instance of revolutionary intervention. One of the reasons for its success is that feminists have supplemented their marxism with other analytic systems developed in the sixties and seventies, among them structuralism and semiotics.

iii

Before you can set about changing the world, you need to define it in such a way that changes are possible. You do this by conceiving of it not as a physical essence (a bundle of atoms held together by gravity) but as a social system (a bundle of categories held together by custom). What marxists hope to change is not the nature of human life − birth, copulation and death − but the cultural organisation of it in terms of various categories such as wealth or race, each of which privileges a minority of people and oppresses the majority. The lesson for feminism is obvious. If you want to change the way people think about women in a world dominated by men, you must first discourage the habit of defining 'woman' as an essence whose 'nature' is determined biologically, and whose sole destiny is to reproduce the human species. For that is precisely the ideology − 'anatomy is destiny' − which makes a woman feel it is somehow 'unnatural' of her to place any activity above her reproductive role. It also ensures that men encounter only a little competition at work from a few female 'freaks' and none at all from the majority of 'real' women, who stay at home to bring up families in their 'proper' sphere. In order to change that situation, you have to conceive of 'woman' not as an essence which precedes the social organisation of life, but as a category or construct produced by a society and mediated in the discourses which it circulates about itself. It is not a question of deciding what a woman 'is' by nature, but of examining what she is assumed to be in the society or culture in which she lives, how those assumptions came about, and whose interests they serve. For seeing that different societies 'construct' women in different ways, it is clear that 'woman' − far from being an immutable essence − is in fact a culturally variable construct, which each society produces for particular purposes. Feminists can argue accordingly that the dominant construct of woman in our society was produced originally to serve the interests of a patriarchy. In order to give women more opportunities, therefore, it is not necessary to tamper with their biological nature (although medical technology, by developing contraceptive and *in vitro* fertilisation techniques, tries to do precisely that), but to change the patriarchal construct of woman. And in order to theorise that problem, feminists can turn to structural anthropology and to semiotics, both of which developed from the descriptive linguistics pioneered earlier this century by Ferdinand de Saussure in his *Course in general linguistics* (1916; London, 1960).

A good place to start is with Saussure's conception of language as a system of signs, each of which is made up of a sound-image or 'signifier' and a concept or 'signified'. In different languages, the same signified is indicated by different signifiers, which means that if you confront people with a large graminivorous quadruped they will identify it as a *cheval* if they are French, *Pferd* if German and 'horse' if English; the same animal was *equus* to the Romans and *hippos* to the ancient Greeks. What changes here is not the thing itself but the sound-images or words chosen to denote it. This relationship between signifier and signified, therefore, can be considered 'natural' only by monolingual speakers with no reason to doubt that a horse is a horse is a horse; but polyglots are better placed to understand the arbitrariness of that link between word and thing which makes it possible to say that a horse by any other name would smell as sweet. 'The arbitrariness of the sign' is therefore a fundamental principle in Saussurean linguistics: language is not a representation of reality, but a system of signification – words are not things, but merely signs for things. This is worth bearing in mind if you are looking for a way of discrediting those essentialistic definitions of 'woman' which underpin all talk about what is or is not proper for women to do. Linguistically, 'woman' is a sign, not an essence, and hence whatever meaning that word happens to have does not inhere in it 'naturally' but is conferred upon it by the society which uses it: its meaning is determined by custom or convention. The key to 'woman' is therefore not biology but semiotics, that so-called science of signs which studies what David Saunders calls 'the processes of production and recognition of meanings in society'.[39]

Saussure effected that Copernican revolution which resulted in descriptive linguistics by asking how language works instead of how it develops. Breaking with a dominant philology which held that language study should be based on historical principles and focus on developments in language 'through time' (diachronically), Saussure invented a new linguistics based on the hypothesis that the most important characteristic of language as a system is not the individual histories of the separable items which constitute it but how they interrelate simultaneously (synchronically). In pre-Saussurean philology, for instance, language is conceived of as a collocation of separate sounds, each of which has chànged over the centuries, and the main problem is to explain (by reference to available texts and 'cognate' forms in related languages) how every sound in the language we speak got to be what it is. To describe each sound accurately is the province of phonetics, while philology plots the mutations of sounds through history. So whereas phoneticians describe the 'o' in 'stone', for instance, as a diphthong and transcribe it by the phonetic symbol [oʊ], philologists reconstruct its trajectory back through [o:] and [ɔ:] to the [a:] of Old English *stan*, at which point they run out of texts and are obliged to resort to conjectural Germanic and Indo-European ancestors. The diachronic chains of sounds produced as a result of these phonological investigations are paralleled elsewhere in nineteenth-century philology, for example in etymology and semantics, to which the greatest monument is the *Oxford English dictionary* (based 'on historical principles'). But they are paralleled also in fields outside language study, and most famously in Darwinian evolution, which has a similar fascination with pedigrees and inscrutable origins. Indeed, all such activities – including investigations into the 'sources' of literary works, and textual studies whose stemmata trace the 'correct' descent of texts through mazes of corrupt manuscripts and slovenly editions – testify to the same conviction that because the present is the product of the past, how you are regarded depends very much on where you have come from. The fact that this type of diachronic scholarship achieved some of its greatest successes at the same time as Victorian patriarchy flourished prompts speculation as to whether a diachronic fascination with origins and lineage signifies a displacement of patrilineal anxieties from family life into scholarship, it being a well-known fact that it is a wise child that knows its own father.

A basic component in the synchronic analysis of language is the phoneme, which is the name given to the smallest unit of sound by which a change of meaning is effected. The word 'stone', for instance, contains three phonemes: /st/, /o/ and /n/. Phonemes are the distinctive features of language viewed synchronically. Their identity is determined not by their history but by the company they keep, and they maintain their identity by standing in opposition to rival elements. Looked at from a synchronically phonemic (instead of a diachronically phonetic) point of view, the word 'stone' is what it is not because it developed from *stan* but because it differs from a number of similar-sounding words such as 'tone', 'stun' and 'stole'. Each of the constituent phonemes of 'stone' stands in opposition to other phonemes, the substitution of any one of which would totally alter the meaning produced by its conjunction with the two remaining phonemes. 'Stone' is 'stone', in other words, because the phoneme /st/ is not /b/, /f/ or /m/, the substitution of which would result in 'bone', 'phone' and 'moan'; because the phoneme /o/ is not /ai/, /er/ or /u/ (which would give 'stain', 'stern' and 'stun'); and because the phoneme /n/ is not /k/, /l/ or /t/ ('stoke', 'stole' and 'stoat').

Synchronic linguistics describes language as a self-regulating system which tolerates transformation without ever losing its equilibrium. The system is always complete at any synchronic moment: the language we speak nowadays is phonemically as intact as the one spoken by Chaucer, despite phonetic differences between the two. Its constituent elements are held apart in binary opposition to one another, but congregate in the production of meaning. Everything is related to everything else (as in the best-known appropriation of this model, the environmental ecosystem), and no phoneme is more important than any other. The production of meaning is dependent on permutations of phonemes, none of which has meaning alone. This is what makes synchronic linguistics attractive to people who have no professional interest in the subject but are puzzled by other meaning-conferring apparatuses such as literature or myths or social customs, the complexities of which resist systemic definition. The principal lessons to be learned from linguistics by prospective Copernicans in other disciplines are relatively few but extremely important: that the object of enquiry should be wholes rather than parts, and relationships rather than essences; and that the question of how meaning is produced is more important than which meaning is correct.

There is obviously much to interest feminists in a project like linguistics, which determined from the outset to be 'descriptive' in contradistinction to the 'prescriptive' grammars it sought to replace. Its policy of taking up questions of value later rather than sooner (if at all) is implied in the claim that, linguistically speaking, no piece of language is intrinsically more valuable than any other, and that different 'contexts of situation' promote different criteria of appropriateness and efficacy. If value does not inhere in texts but is conferred upon them, the distinction between 'literature' and 'non-literature' is without foundation; there is merely 'writing' (*écriture*), some of which gets called 'literature' by people whose interests it satisfies. This is useful to know when confronted by the jibe that most women are not capable of creating literature, and that the few who are have been acknowledged already. A shift in emphasis from 'literature' to *écriture* permits attention to be given to what earlier critics consider marginal or subliterary forms, such as letters and journals, and to just about any piece of discursive prose which has something to say about women. Mahl and Koon's anthology of 'English Women Writers before 1800' is not the usual assemblage of poems plus excerpts from plays and novels.[40] On the contrary, it includes selections from Bathsua Makin's *An essay to revive the ancient education of gentlewomen* (1673) as well as from a tract on the virtues of breastfeeding, *The Countess of Lincoln's nursurie* (1622). People who believe that this kind of thing would never have been included if there hadn't been a dearth of 'real' literature to choose from can be told that a survey of women's writing is obliged to be descriptive rather than prescriptive, and to take account of what women actually wrote instead of berating them for what they didn't write. If the conditions in which women have written in the past were more conducive to the production of letters and diaries and children's stories than to epic poems and five-act tragedies, then the former will necessarily occupy a more central place in a literary history designed to represent women than in one designed to represent men. To speak of 'women's writing' enables feminists to bypass problems of value raised in androcentric criticism by the term 'women's literature'.

The demonstration that linguistic meaning is produced by a system of articulated differences is likely to interest anybody investigating the production of social meaning by and for men and women in societies like ours, where the gendering of sexual difference into masculine and feminine components does not result in the equilibrium predicted by the linguistic model. On the contrary, in the binary system which structures sexual difference, one of the paired terms is always privileged, and almost invariably it is the masculine one. Saussure was careful to distinguish the egalitarian nature of binary opposition at the phonemic level of language from those hierarchically structured pairs encountered in other dualistic types of analysis. 'A difference generally implies positive terms between which the difference is set up', he said, 'but in language there are only differences *without positive terms*.'[41] The phonemes /r/ and /c/ are equal and opposite when they compete systemically for the company of /a/ and /t/; it is only at another level in the signifying process – the semantic – that the phonemic differentiation between 'cat' and 'rat' is subject to hierarchical preferences. If it is true that binary terms tend to be locked together not in horizontal complementarity (equal and opposite) but in vertical hierarchy (superior and inferior), then 'complementarity' is unmasked as a myth which conceals the fact that one of such pairs is always favoured at the expense of the other. This has serious consequences for the construction of male–female relationships, given the antiquity and ubiquity of binary thought processes. The earliest recorded list of binary opposites is attributed by Aristotle to the Pythagoreans: it sets 'male' against 'female', 'right' against 'left' and 'good' against 'evil' in such a way that the list appears to be tacitly promoting a first-term sequence (male/right/good) at the expense of a second-term sequence (female/left/evil).[42] The slide here from structural parity into semantic disparity signals the presence of another force at work, which first centralises masculinity by marginalising femininity, and then valorises the former by denigrating the latter. 'Theoretically subordinated to the concept of masculinity', writes Shoshana Felman, 'the woman is viewed by the man as *his* opposite, that is to say, as *his* other, the negative of the positive, and not, in her own right, different, other, Otherness itself.'[43]

Felman's language echoes Simone de Beauvoir's classic exposition of alterity (otherness, 'otherhood') as 'a fundamental category of human thought', resulting from a duality of Self and Other 'as primordial as consciousness itself'.[44] What begins as an existential problem for each of us individually as we try to reconcile the 'ipseity' of the Self with the 'alterity' of the Other becomes a political problem for us collectively when we have to decide what constitute society's Self and Other. If Self is white then black is Other; if Self is heterosexual, homosexuals are Other; and so on. Whatever the pair, the Other is made to feel apart from the whole rather than a part of it, and ends up subordinated and oppressed. Beauvoir starts from the insight that societies are organised on the assumption that man is Self and woman Other, and that the consequences are always deleterious to women. The reason for this is that the Self treats the Other as either a supplement or a threat. If woman is conceived of as a supplement to man, she becomes the receptacle either of what he doesn't want ('weaknesses'), or what he cannot have, like Clara Middleton in George Meredith's *The egoist* (1879), who 'completed' Willoughby, and 'added the softer lines wanting to his portrait before the world'.[45] The 'supplementary' woman may find herself set on a pedestal as the object of chivalric attentions, 'worshipped', in return for which she is expected to surrender her autonomy and see it as her destiny to serve the man's interests (as mistress, muse, wife, or power-behind-the-throne). If, however, the Other cannot be cajoled into supplementarity, she is credited with the same status as uppity niggers in racist manifestations of the Self–Other dialogue, and becomes the victim of the Self's misogyny, of which pornography is the art form, and rape and murder the unsublimated practice.

This binary analysis of male–female relations in terms of Self and Other has important consequences for literary studies because of its bearing on how and why we read. If it is true that the only texts which are considered to be literature in a patriarchal society are those which are either wholly androcentric or not so gynocentric as to be troublesome, then women may find them alienating to read – so much so, in fact, as to advocate replacing them with a rival set of texts which women feel they can 'identify with'. But there are drawbacks in defining reading as an act of recognition in quite so narrow a sense: do we read only in order to fortify the Self, and never to experience the Other? In the liberal humanist tradition, books are seen as constituting vistas on the Other as well as mirrors of the Self, and it was not until instant gratification was elevated into a cultural ideal in the 1960s that much notice was taken of the view that the only books worth studying are those one can 'identify with' immediately. The purpose of reading promiscuously is to acquire certain experiences vicariously which are unavailable in one's everyday life. The reason why they are not available may be a personal disinclination to risk involvement in some of the extreme situations described in books, or (as marxists prefer to think) it may be the result of a lack of opportunity to lead a rich and varied life except at second-hand through substitutes for the real thing. But if the Self happens to be female and the Other male, and reading is construed solely as reading-for-self-identity, the reading of androtexts poses a dilemma. 'The real question', according to Josephine Donovan, 'is not whether a woman *can* identify with the subjective consciousness of the self if it is male, but whether she *should*, given her own political and social environment.'[46]

Politicised in this way, to read promiscuously is to read perfidiously, and to be compelled to do so by a patriarchal education system which favours androtexts is an injustice to women. In such conditions, the only authentic reader is Fetterley's 'resisting' reader, who refuses to let herself be 'immasculated' into the sort of token male who succeeds by apeing male ways of reading, and instead gets a purchase on androcentric classics by reading them against the grain. The feared alternative, especially for women who turn out to be 'good at English', is to end up in that condition of divided consciousness described by Elaine Showalter, being at once 'daughters of the male tradition' which asks them to be 'rational, marginal and grateful' and 'sisters in a new women's movement' which requires them to 'renounce the pseudo-success of token womanhood, and the ironic masks of academic debate'.[47] As a moderate, Showalter thinks that the gap which opens for an educated woman reader between a Self made up of female-specific 'experience' and an Other which is androcentric could be closed by the invention of a new kind of discourse which would integrate intelligence with experience. Separatists, of course, take a much less sanguine view.

What tends to get overlooked in discussions of this matter is the fact that disaffection from dominant cultural practices is by no means unique to women, as any history of dissenting traditions would show by way of contextualising all those twentieth-century male 'outsiders' who have taken up an adversary position to their own culture in order to write. Long before Fetterley learnt from marxist criticism that reading can be an oppositional practice, Lionel Trilling was explaining to liberal humanists the advantages of cultivating the 'opposing self', on the grounds that 'quarrels with the culture' are a 'necessity not only of the self but of culture'.[48] As for the assumption that to designate an Other is necessarily to denigrate it, this is certainly discredited by the way in which the concept of alterity is used in literary history in order to protect (say) a fourteenth-century Other from abuse by a modernising twentieth-century Self.[49] Nor is the Other a demeaning concept to Linda Bamber, who argues that in Shakespeare the feminine-as-Other is 'for the most part a form of external reality, an embodiment of the world and not merely a vessel for what the psyche rejects'.[50] By showing that 'the Self is privileged in tragedy, the Other in comedy' she avoids a couple of errors in feminist criticism of Shakespeare. One is to regard the presence of high-spirited female characters in the comedies as evidence that Shakespeare must have been a feminist (which is what his reputation for myriad-mindedness would suggest: whatever interests people can always be 'found' in Shakespeare). The other error is to argue from the way women are represented in the tragedies – the characterisation of Cleopatra tends to be somehow overlooked – that Shakespeare was as much a misogynist as the next man, as some of his sonnets 'prove'.

The advantage of working from Beauvoir's binary analysis of Self and Other rather than from revisionist versions of it such as Bamber's is that it provides an excellent base for the view that woman is always constructed negatively in an androcentric society, and always has been. In the Aristotelian tradition, a woman is not a woman but a man *manqué*, an *animal occasionatum* who is defined by what she lacks.[51] Created second according to a Hebrew myth which Christians inherited as holy writ in the book of Genesis, every woman enters history with a piece missing, whether it is a head according to St Paul or a penis according to Sigmund Freud.[52] Whatever the deficiency, men think of themselves as uniquely qualified to supplement it, provided women show their gratitude by submissiveness. The binary opposition between Self and Other manifests itself therefore in our value system as possession versus lack, and becomes the generative matrix for a series of metaphors which constitute variations on the same theme. 'Lack' is troped as feminine 'absence' by contrast with masculine 'presence', 'invisibility' as against 'visibility', 'silence' as against 'voice', 'gap' as against 'text', the gap being in semiotic terms a marker denoting the presence of an absence. It is taken to be axiomatic that the absence of the feminine from discourses which are subsequently masculine by default has come about not fortuitously but as a result of acts of exclusion. The Other, that is to say, has not been accidentally 'lost' but deliberately 'erased', and the business of a feminist criticism is to reinscribe the feminine Other in a discourse still dominated by a masculine Self which, scandalously, has claimed to speak for women as well as men while in fact speaking solely for men.

The subjection of women, therefore, is brought about not by their 'natural' inferiority but by their classification as intrinsically inferior by a male-dominated culture they cannot avoid living in. The rival forces which compete discursively for the possession of 'woman' used to be called 'nature' and 'custom', or (by those with a taste for a euphuistic turn of phrase) 'nature' and 'nurture'. Nowadays the pair is labelled Nature and Culture, which Claude Lévi-Strauss has made the most famous binary opposition in structuralist thought. Nature is the way things are, and Culture what we make them out to be. 'Custom', Bathsua Makin noted in 1673, 'hath a mighty influence: it hath the force of Nature itself.'[53] This is because in growing up we internalise cultural conventions so well that they become 'second nature' to us, and therefore even to conceive of breaking with them seems 'unnatural'. For it is characteristic of Culture to be passed off as Nature, especially by dominant groups who resort to this tactic in order to police human behaviour and keep other groups subordinate. The relevance to feminism of the Nature–Culture distinction is epitomised in Simone de Beauvoir's aphorism, 'One is not born, but rather becomes, a woman.'[54] What enables a girl to become a woman is not simply the pubertal transformation of her body (Nature) but the socialising processes of Culture which influence how she thinks of herself and try to dictate what she ought to do with her life. Women are not inferior by Nature but inferiorised by Culture: they are acculturated into inferiority. If 'woman' were simply a female sexual essence in the domain of Nature – a unified, transhistorical and constant subject ('the eternal feminine') – she would be able to speak her own meanings and experiences, provided she were able to communicate in a language free from patriarchal interference. But 'woman' is not an essence but a construct in the domain of patriarchal Culture, a dispersed subject, historically variable, socially feminised, and a site on which masculine meanings get spoken and masculine desires enacted. The corollary of all this, of course, is that if women are not essences but constructs, the same must be true also of men, which means that what feminists are opposed to cannot logically be men as such (Nature) but rather the male supremacist role conferred on men by Culture in a patriarchy.

'Is female to male as nature is to culture?' Sherry B. Ortner once asked before reporting that the answer to that question ought to be 'No', and that things won't improve for women until everybody concedes as much.[55] The form of her question (female : male = nature : culture) is structuralist in its assumption that binary oppositions get replicated at different levels in a system, and that the relationship between the two constituent elements of any such pair will be homologous with that of other pairs. 'Homology' is the name given to similarities of relationship. When Lévi-Strauss appropriated structural linguistics as a model for structural anthropology, and wrote that kinship structures can be explained 'only by treating marriage regulations and kinship systems as a kind of language', he was thinking analogically and hoping that a linguistics-based structural anthropology would illuminate the workings of kinship systems in the way that systemic linguistics had illuminated the workings of language. But when he went on to observe that in a kinship system it is 'the *women of the group*, who are *circulated* between clans . . . in place of the *words of the group*, which are *circulated* between individuals', the similarity he had in mind between women and words as currency in communication systems was that of relationship: homologically, women : clans = words : individuals.[56] In feminist discourse it is common to encounter homological equations between sexual practices and cultural formations, most often by way of protest against oppressively phallocratic homologies like the one which structures St Paul's defence of marital inequality on the grounds that 'the husband is the head of the wife, even as Christ is the head of the Church' (Ephesians 5.23). The conjunction of sexuality and politics in the key term 'sexual politics' licenses a good deal of homological freeplay. Marks and de Courtivron draw attention to the way French feminists ridicule 'the male erection, the male preoccupation with getting it up, keeping it up, and the ways in which the life and death of the penis are projected into other aspects of culture'.[57] Power structures replicate coital postures, according to Eva Figes, who thinks that 'the idea of submission is inherent in the way we make love, man on top, woman underneath'.[58] Resistance to phallic domination begins therefore with a rejection of the submissionary posture, which is why feminist books and journals have been published with titles like *Women on top*, *Off our backs*, *Up from under* and *The turn of the screwed*.[59]

Feminist treatments of clitoridectomy − the ritual excision of the clitoris − illustrate how a semiotic style of analysis can operate homologically with a variety of texts, some of them literary, to link the microstructure of sexual practices to the macrostructure of sexual politics. Clitoridectomy is the subject of a gruesome chapter in Mary Daly's *Gyn/ecology*, where it is used to illustrate the point 'that androcracy is the State of Atrocity, where atrocities are normal, ritualized, repeated'.[60] Thematised in this way, clitoridectomy can be accommodated into fiction either directly as a barbarity practised by 'primitive' peoples, which is how Margaret Laurence handles it in *This side Jordan* (1960), or more obliquely as a civilised atrocity perpetrated by the medical profession and designed to control 'unruly' women, as in Conan Doyle's displacement narrative about the 'case' of the sexually adventurous Lady Sannox (1894), who had 'a broad V-shaped piece' cut surgically from what is called her 'under lip' because her husband thought the operation 'morally' necessary.[61] But if clitoridectomy is homologised instead of thematised, attention shifts from the horrors of the act — performed without anaesthetics by women on girls as a 'purification' rite — to the semiotic status of the clitoris as a signifier of female sexuality, and to its place in other signifying practices by means of which an androcentric society constructs its idea of woman. Thus clitoridectomy is taken by Gayatri Chakravorty Spivak to be metonymic of how woman is defined (in what she calls our 'uterine social organization') as the possessor of a necessary womb for childbearing and a correspondingly 'superfluous' clitoris.[62] For Spivak, clitoridectomy figures homologously as the bloody and agonising enactment of what civilised patriarchies achieve less painfully but no less outrageously through legal and medical apparatuses which, by defining female sexuality in terms of reproduction (womb) instead of pleasure (clitoris), manage to excise female sexuality as a non-reproductive, autonomous pleasure. Consequently, 'repression of the clitoris as the signifier of the sexed subject', writes Spivak, 'operates the specific oppression of women'. And the effects of that repression are reproduced not only in Freudian psychology, where women are designated immature until they have learned to forsake the pleasures of clitoral stimulation for what Anne Koedt calls 'the myth of the vaginal orgasm', but also in other domains, such as lexicography and literature.[63] It is significant that Henley and Farmer have no entry for 'clitoris' in their dictionary of *Slang and its analogues* (London, 1893), although they manage to fill seventeen columns with ingenious euphemisms for 'cunt' (an entry which they locate under *m* for 'monosyllable', a taxonomical feat which tells its own story of repression by displacement). And it is equally significant that the clitoris should be hard to find in books once so notorious for their sexual explicitness as to be banned, despite the literary fashion (originating in Renaissance love poetry) for itemising *blasons* which fragment the female body lubriciously and offer it piecemeal to the male reader for voyeuristic excitement, as in Spenser's 'Epithalamion' (1595):

> Her forehead yvory white,
> Her cheekes lyke apples which the sun hath rudded,
> Her lips lyke cherryes charming men to byte,
> Her brest like to a bowle of creame vncrudded,
> Her paps lyke lyllies budded.   (lines 172–6)

But as Robert Scholes discovered, the clitoris is curiously absent from
the numerous descriptions of female genitalia in *Fanny Hill* (1749),
except perhaps the one in which Fanny is said to have a 'soft fleshy
excrescence' displaced to roughly where Ernst Grafenberg and his
followers expect to find the fabled G spot.[64] As for Lady Chatterley,
if she ever had a clitoris it escaped Mellors' digital examination of her
genital region, and consequently their lovemaking never induced in him
that sexual nausea he experienced with his wife, who was one of those
'old rampers [who] have beaks between their legs'.[65] Tracking
homological representations such as these is part of a feminist semiotics
which, by investigating how men and women 'read' one another, shows
here some of the ways in which an oppressively androcentric
conception of female sexuality gets 'inscribed' in cultural practices,
manifesting itself not only in literal mutilations of the female body but
also in those symbolic mutilations which first prescribe norms for
female sexuality and then classify departures from them as lesbian
'deviance' or heterosexual 'nymphomania', the latter being Lady
Sannox's unspecified infirmity.

So successfully has the clitoral been repressed that even recent French
feminist psychoanalytic criticism, which has taught us to be acutely
aware of such matters, has tended (in Naomi Schor's phrase) 'to
valorize the vagina' at the expense of the clitoris. It has done so as a
result of theorising the production of avant-garde texts (*écriture
féminine*); and in Schor's view, this 'vaginal' theory of textual
production needs to be complemented by a 'clitoral' hermeneutics
which would focus on details in the textual body, specifically 'those
details of the female anatomy which have been generally ignored by
male critics and which significantly influence our reading of the
texts in which they appear'.[66] The crucial concept here is
'complementarity', for to characterise the new 'clitoral' project of
textual interpretation as being somehow opposed to the old 'vaginal'
one of textual production would be to remain trapped in the patriarchal
conception of the clitoral and the vaginal as mutually incompatible
vehicles of female sexuality, one legitimate and the other not.

The advantage of a homological method of investigation is that it
avoids problems associated with that 'specular' model of literary
enquiry which treats art as some sort of mirror to life and expects
literature to reflect what goes on around it. A recent example of the
specular model in a fairly pristine form is to be found in Patricia Otto
Klaus's extremely useful bibliographical essay on the ways in which

women are represented in Victorian fiction. She calls her essay 'Women in the mirror'; and although she is aware of what she calls 'distortions' caused by the novelists' obligation to be entertaining and instructive – and is willing to concede that what we find in fiction is 'a composite of reality filtered through the artist's perceptions and abilities, and our own reading' – she is not sufficiently troubled by any of these considerations to question the status of literature as evidence in a social history of women. Somehow, 'the sensitive scholar' will manage to overcome such obstacles and treat Victorian fiction as 'a very special source for understanding the Victorian woman'.[67] Significantly, she makes no reference to Peter Laslett's sceptical observations on the uses of literary evidence in sociological studies. The trouble with literature as a documentary source for social historians and sociologists, Laslett points out, is the way it mixes graphic and plausible details with 'irremediable vagueness' as to their representativeness: you never know whether the memorable details are typical or quite extraordinary. Exactly what is to be learned from a reading of *Pamela*, for example, about the conditions of eighteenth-century servant girls? What Richardson gives us in that novel, Laslett argues, is 'commentary on tendencies rather than on present realities, reflections to be shared by his readers rather than mirror-like reflectiveness of the society which they shared together'.[68] Clearly, there are drawbacks in treating literature as if it were some kind of pre-sociological sociology, and as if social realities were simply reflected in artistic forms.

This is a difficulty encountered by any feminist who wants to incorporate English literature into women's studies: what is it to be studied as? When Marlene Springer read through the collection of essays she was editing on women in 'English and American life and literature' she observed that 'facts frequently refute the literature to an abnormal degree'.[69] This may well be because literary texts canonise the idiosyncratic. If you had to write about the position of women in England in the early twentieth century, for instance, and the only documents you had were the novels of Virginia Woolf, what would you conclude? The answer, Jane Marcus suggests, is 'that marriage was a primitive institution in decline; that many women perceived male sexuality as rape; that lesbianism and homosexuality were widespread; that spinsterhood, aunthood, sisterhood, and female friendship were women's most important roles; that motherhood and wifehood were Victorian relics'.[70] None of this need bother people who study Woolf in author-based literature courses, where everything in the novels can be imbricated with biographical revelations and thus psychologised, or approached formalistically so as to focus on the technical expertise with which she deploys what are taken to be characteristic themes in her work. Problems arise only if the body of writings labelled 'Woolf' gets shifted from the domain of literature into some adjacent domain such as history, because each discipline constitutes its object according to different linguistic and interpretative conventions. In the domain of literature, for instance, writers can say anything they like provided they say it well. This is because liberal humanist readers of literature are more impressed by its 'performative' characteristics – the illusion it creates that its constitutive utterances are self-sufficient enactments of its meaning – than by those 'constative' features of its language which place it in a relation of correspondence to external reality, and therefore permit questions to be asked about its representational accuracy. But in the domain of history, the constativeness of literary language is valued more highly than its performativeness. 'Literary texts', the Marxist–Feminist Literature Collective concludes, 'cannot give us a knowledge of the social formation; but they do give us something of equal importance in analysing culture, an imaginary representation of real relations.'[71] How those representations come to be made and validated is a more immediately interesting question than whether or not historians or sociologists think them correct.

iv

Binary systems which sort people into winners and losers or oppressors and oppressed tend to be imagined in two dominant forms. One is a 'vertical' model which, by a sort of pun, visualises hierarchy as the placing of a 'higher' above a lower (class or race or whatever), and puts 'top people' with supertax problems above 'the bottom of the heap of humanity' which starves on the streets of Calcutta. The other is a 'horizontal' model which has a centre occupied by an élite, and *hoi polloi* banished to its margins: this is the organising trope for traditional hostilities between the metropolis and the provinces, or the mother country and her colonies. Saussurean linguistics provides the basis on which to mount a critique of 'vertical' modes of oppression by unmasking that myth of equal-and-opposite complementarity with which they conceal their hierarchical orderings. How would one go about dismantling a centre-and-margins mode of oppression?

Each of the social groups from whose underprivileged conditions feminists have troped the oppression of women is itself marginalised by the centring of an exclusive hegemony which blacks identify as 'ethnocentric', Third World peoples as 'Eurocentric' and women as 'androcentric'. According to Lester F. Ward, who introduced the term, 'the androcentric theory is the view that the male sex is primary and the female secondary', and 'that all things center, as it were, about the male'.[72] Feminist usage of the word is common after 1911, when Charlotte Perkins Gilman subtitled *The man-made world* (a book dedicated to Ward) 'Our androcentric culture'. And although rival terms have sometimes been proposed unsuccessfully – in *Three guineas* (1938) Woolf calls our ideology 'inveterately anthropocentric' – the word which displaced it eventually was 'phallocentric', which has a somewhat specialised sense in the psychoanalytic theory of Jacques Lacan, the relevance of which to feminism was first made clear to anglophone readers in an influential essay published by Anthony Wilden in 1972.[73] The negative task of feminist criticism is therefore to dismantle androcentrism (or phallocentrism). And that job has been made considerably easier by the deconstructive philosophy of Jacques Derrida, whose writings constitute as powerful an attack on the mystique of the centre in conceptual systems as Saussure's do on the mystique of origins.

Derrida says he set himself the task of investigating 'the law which governed . . . the desire for the center in the constitution of structure', and concluded that 'the center had no natural locus'.[74] It is not an irreducible presence like Mt Everest, which is antecedent to all talk about it. By contrast, the 'centre' as a concept in classical systems of thought is merely a construct which is brought into existence by the privileging of some signifiers at the expense of others, and for reasons which turn out to be in the interests of those who do the privileging. So whereas the highest mountain in the Himalayas is the signified which validates the signifier 'Everest', there is no transcendental signified which validates the signifier 'centre'. 'In the absence of a center or origin', Derrida explains, 'everything became discourse.' Once again, Saussurean linguistics provides the key insight, for the differential system which constitutes language at the phonemic level operates perfectly well without reference to a centre. There is no 'master' phoneme or set of phonemes which constitutes the organisational matrix of language as a signifying practice; instead, language articulates itself differentially by perpetually bringing into play an infinite number of phoneme substitutions. And therefore what is true of language in particular is held to be true of discourses in general, which traditionally have been organised around some transcendental centre — such as God or Nature or Man — whose allegedly extra-textual presence is believed to legitimate all subsequent enquiries. The deconstructive endeavour is therefore to 'decentre' all such discourses. The liberating effect of such a manoeuvre is to recognise that what presents itself as a centre of power which organises the discourse it is embedded in is in fact merely a function or product of that discourse.

Three types of centring come under damaging scrutiny in Derridean analysis: 'phonocentrism' in linguistics, 'logocentrism' in philosophy, and 'phallocentrism' in psychoanalysis. Phonocentrism privileges the voice (*phone*) in such a way as to consolidate the illusion that speech is more natural than writing. It leads us to believe that by comparison with writing (which some civilisations have managed to get along quite well without, and which in any case has to be learned laboriously) speech is spontaneous, authentic and unmediated. Against this position Derrida argues that because the voice has no meaning except through the medium of language, and because the phonemic permutations which constitute language can be explained only as a system of writing using letters (*gramma*), we need to move beyond Saussure's speech-based linguistics and into an alternative and writing-based 'grammatology'. Western civilisation has made the mistake of supposing that writing depends parasitically on speech. But on the contrary, it is speech which depends on writing — not the writing that we do with pens or typewriters, but the phonemic 'writing' that writes our speech for us before we speak, that prior activity of phonemic differentiation which Derrida calls 'the arche-writing [*archi-écriture*] that opens speech itself'.[75] But how did we come to misconceive the order of speech and writing? The answer to that lies not in linguistics but in philosophy, which has been dominated traditionally by a 'metaphysics of presence' which Derrida calls 'logocentrism' (from *logos*, the spoken word, reason, God), and of which phonocentrism is symptomatic. The phonocentric fallacy is to believe that 'behind' every piece of writing is a voice denoting a presence which guarantees and authenticates it in the way that the tallest Himalayan mountain guarantees and authenticates the signifier 'Everest'. Homologically, 'centre' is to discourse as 'presence' is to being. If we are ever to succeed in decentring the structures of thought in which we are trapped by the logocentric fallacy that there is a First Cause of being and meaning, we shall have to surrender our nostalgia for what Derrida calls 'full presence, the reassuring foundation, the origin and the end of the game', and put at risk our humanism by questioning the logocentric premises which sustain it.[76] For humanism places man at the centre of world history, making the decisions which will determine his future. And women are not man.

To decentre logocentrism would involve reversing the values placed on each component in the binary terms which constitute it. 'Writing' would thus become privileged at the expense of 'speech', 'absence' at the expense of 'presence'; 'appearance' would dislodge 'essence', 'the unconscious' 'consciousness', and so on. Somewhere along the line the pair 'male–female' would get rewritten as 'female–male', thus deprivileging the order condoned by an androcentric society which, in psychoanalytic terms, is 'phallocentric'. Since the word 'phallus' is interchangeable with 'penis' in ordinary usage, it is important to remember that this is not the case in that branch of psychoanalysis which concerns itself with psychosexual development, that is, with the unconscious formation of sexuality during infancy and childhood. In the discourse of psychoanalysis, the word 'phallus' does not denote the anatomical organ 'penis', but is rather the signifier or symbol of what we desire but lack, irrespective of which sex we happen to be. So for Jacques Lacan, whose writings constitute the ground on which current debates between feminism and psychoanalysis are conducted, the phallus is a sexually neutral 'signifier of desire . . . the ultimate significative object, which appears when all the veils are lifted'.[77] It is therefore the key term for explaining the psychic organisation of such things as our sense of possession and lack, or presence and absence, in all aspects of human experience, including of course the sexual, where it is said to operate as an asexual third term in relation to which femininity is differentiated from masculinity. Psychoanalytically speaking, therefore, not even the most virile of men possesses 'the phallus', because his penis merely symbolises the phallus he lacks. The particular plight of a woman, therefore, is not that she lacks a penis as such, but that by not having one she is deprived of the means to symbolise her lack: boys lack the phallus, but girls lack even the lack of the phallus.

Difficulties arise, however, with this attempt to desynonymise 'penis' and 'phallus', partly because common usage synonymises them, and partly because common sense tells us (as it told Jane Gallop) that ' "phallus" cannot function as signifier in ignorance of "penis" ', and that the very selection of the phallus as the ultimate signifier of desire indicates a male bias in the system of symbolisation.[78] It is easy to see why the penis, on the other hand, might get chosen as a symbol for such purposes, as its involuntary erections and detumescences make it the most visible natural indicator of the presence or absence of desire. But to say this is merely to confirm the presence of androcentric bias in the system. For from a feminist point of view, the very idea that something is validated by virtue of its ability to be seen is symptomatic of a masculine psychic economy, which privileges sight because the male genitals are visible in a way that the female are not. Women, by contrast, keep in touch with their sexuality by means of a correspondingly more 'tactile' psychic organisation: 'so much male love poetry celebrates the glance of an eye', Ellen Moers notes, whereas 'women's love poems thrive on the touch'.[79] But in any case, there is something disingenuous in claiming that the phallus is asexual in psychoanalytic usage, when clearly it has been selected on account of properties associated with the penis. We cannot imagine a phallus without thinking of a penis, and this is why (as Gallop remarks with her characteristic raunchiness) 'feminists find that central, transcendental phallus particularly hard to swallow'.[80]

The problem originates of course with Freud, and has resulted in varying intensities of dissent among psychoanalysts who feel (as Ernest Jones did in 1927) that 'men analysts have been led to adopt an unduly phallo-centric view' of female psychosexual development.[81] In the opinion of Juliet Mitchell, who argued in her first book 'that a rejection of psychoanalysis and of Freud's works is fatal for feminism', Freud thought that psychoanalysis could hardly avoid being phallocentric in a society organised along patriarchal lines: 'if psychoanalysis is phallocentric, it is because the human social order that it perceives refracted through the individual human subject is patrocentric'.[82] And a similar defence of Lacan's phallocentricity is made by Jacqueline Rose when she writes that to construct male and female sexuality by reference to the phallic term 'reveals that sexual identity is socially constituted rather than naturally given'.[83] But a radical feminist more interested in changing the world of psychoanalysis than in understanding it would find phallocentrism symptomatic of logocentrism, with the phallus taking the place of the *logos* in a manoeuvre neatly described by Derrida's portmanteau word 'phallogocentrism' ('It is one and the same system', Derrida remarked in 1973: 'the erection of a paternal logos . . . and of the phallus as "privileged signifier" ').[84] And if that is the case − if women are indeed victims of some sort of collusion between a logocentric conception of knowledge and a phallocentric conception of sexuality – then the more feminists who ally themselves with deconstructive analysis the better. For only on the far side of deconstruction will it be possible to escape domination by the law of the logos as administered under the aegis of the phallus.

Exactly what form a 'post-phallogocentrism' might take prompts utopian speculations. 'What would become of logocentrism, of the great philosophical systems, of world order in general', asks Hélène Cixous, 'if . . . it were to come out in a new day that the logocentric project had always been, undeniably, to *found* (fund) phallocentrism, to insure for masculine order a rationale equal to history itself?' Her answer to that question – 'all the stories would have to be told differently' – is pertinent to anybody who has pondered Anne Elliot's observation in Jane Austen's *Persuasion* (1818) that 'men have had every advantage of us [women] in telling their own story'.[85] Just how far deconstructionist methods are likely to facilitate the telling of women's own story depends on whether feminism is willing to maintain the same fastidious selectiveness in its dealings with deconstruction as has characterised its eclectic encounters with marxism and structuralism.

In view of their preoccupation with giving women a 'voice' after centuries of enforced silence, feminists would appear to have less to gain from Derrida's attack on phonocentrism than from his attack on phallocentrism. The grammatological alternative to phonocentrism may well be a more attractive proposition to men than it is to women, who believe they have not yet experienced the fullness of speech, let alone its excess, and who therefore may wish to enjoy the satisfactions of 'epireading' women writers for a little longer before becoming 'graphireaders'. I take these terms from Denis Donoghue.[86] 'Epireaders' (from *epos*, 'voice') recall the silent author as a voice which speaks the text they are reading; 'graphireaders' (from *graphos*, 'writing') have no contact at all with the author of the text because the words which constitute it are seen as being themselves the originating source of meaning and not (as in the case of epireading) transcriptions of an antecedent and authorial voice. Everybody in our culture is an epireader until taught graphireading by structuralists and deconstructionists. Donoghue's distinction enables us to see that one of the reasons why English studies is now in turmoil is that liberal humanists are much more at ease listening to an 'epitext' than observing a 'graphitext'. But a gender-conscious critic might note that Donoghue — dealing, as he does, almost entirely with male writers — regards the problem of authorial 'absence' and 'silence' as principally the product of reading practices: if you epiread a text, you will hear the voice of its author; if not, not.

He does not argue, as a feminist might, that presence or absence (voice or silence) are determined by what kind of speaking positions are available at the time of writing; and that in an androcentric society, *epos* poses difficulties for women writers long before readers of either sex decide whether to be epireaders or graphireaders.

In so far as deconstruction is capable of being described, it operates by putting everything into question, including the normal operations for putting things into question. As Derrida practises it, there is no deconstructive 'method' as such which can be applied to this or that text; there is merely a series of different occasions on which we observe Derrida engaging in a deconstructive process. It attracts the attention of people who want to change the world because it can be used to such devastating effect on those presuppositions which make the world the way it is, for it replicates at the textual level a desire for perpetual revolution. But it is treacherous to handle. For since there is no position which is not deconstructible, and no deconstructed position which is not further deconstructible, you cannot use it in order to wipe out the opposition and expect to remain intact yourself. In this respect, feminists are no better placed than others who try to soften deconstruction by appropriating carefully selected bits of it, because nobody can tolerate the indiscriminate interrogating entailed in 'hard' deconstruction. To look to deconstruction for ways of decentring masculine constructions of reality, and to do so with a view to centring a feminist construction of reality, is to engage merely in 'soft' deconstruction. 'Deconstruction is not simply a strategic reversal of categories which otherwise remain distinct and unaffected', Christopher Norris points out. 'It seeks to undo both a given order of priorities *and* the very system of conceptual opposition that makes that order possible.'[87] Questioning the priorities of a phallocratic order makes good sense if it oppresses you personally as a woman. But surrendering the system of conceptual opposition may well appear suicidal to women who see no way of theorising feminine specificity except in terms of difference. There is no easy solution to this dilemma. Should women hold on to the concept of difference because to deny women their difference in a patriarchy 'is to inscribe [them] in the law of the same', as Josette Féral puts it: 'same sexuality, same discourse, same economy, same representation, same origin'?[88] Or should they give it up as unproductive because, in Louise Adler's words, 'the articulation of female specificity as constituted as "difference" locates, in a glib gesture, woman as forever oppositional', and 'not all women are oppositional'?[89]

A good deal depends, therefore, on how 'difference' is defined. Deconstruction, as Barbara Johnson reminds us, is more of an 'undoing' than a 'destruction', and manifests itself in 'the careful teasing out of warring forces of signification within the text' – forces which cannot be controlled by a single interpretation. 'A deconstructive reading', she goes on, 'is a reading that analyses the specificity of a text's critical difference from itself', and does so by helping the text to articulate that 'difference from itself which it "knows" but cannot say'.[90] Here deconstruction (which is sometimes called 'post-structuralism', since it developed after structuralism and, as Derrida concedes, could not have done so without it) parts company with structuralism. For whereas structuralism speaks of differences *between*, say, one phoneme and another, or one sex and another, deconstruction concerns itself with differences *within* the 'one' sex or text or whatever.

One way of teasing out these 'endogenous' differences – differences within – is to engage in freeplay with the signifiers and to write in a punning style ('Is a pen a metaphorical penis?') which outsiders find outrageous, thus appropriating for deconstructive purposes the semantic instability made famous by James Joyce in *Finnegans wake* ('How hominous his house, haunt it?').[91] As a disruptive agent, the pun is mightier than the word. This is revealed in the detection of androcentric bias in the word 'history' by transcribing it first as 'his story' and then countering it with the neologism 'herstory' as a feminist righting of a patriarchal wrong.[92] The shift of emphasis in language study to synchronic linguistics condones a new kind of etymologising in which morphemes – those minimal units of meaning – are permitted to interact with one another in ways forbidden by diachronic linguistics, which disparages that kind of thing as 'pseudo-etymology'. Diachronically speaking, 'history' cannot possibly be 'his story' because 'history' derives from the Latin *historia*. The first syllable of *historia* happens to be identical orthographically with the masculine possessive pronoun 'his' (from Old English *hys*), but is certainly not identical with it phonetically, because the sibilant is voiced [z] in 'his' but unvoiced [s] in 'history'. Instead of allowing the meaning of 'history' to be controlled, however, by a diachrony which permits patrilineal anxieties about legitimacy of descent to be displaced into an etymological concern with the 'proper' origins of words, feminists who read 'history' as 'his story' are exercising their deconstructionist right to indulge synchronically in freeplay with the signifiers, and for a worthwhile purpose, namely the unmasking of androcentricity in the very name of a subject which has had far more to say about men than about women. What shocks the virtuous philologist delights the chameleon feminist, who must then take with good grace the diachronic objection that her etymologising is 'mstaken'.[93]

At a molecular level, the transformation of 'history' into 'his story' and its replacement by 'herstory' emblematise the feminist intervention in English studies as both a negative and a positive affair − a deconstructing of androcentrism in order to prepare the ground for a new gynocentrism. In what follows I want to explore in some detail the consequences of both procedures, beginning with feminist manifestations of that 'power of negative thinking' which Herbert Marcuse encourages us to direct against all 'one-dimensional' theories of reality.[94]

3

Dismantling androcentric assumptions

Because language is the most commonly recognised of all those signifying practices which try to ensure that we grow up fully socialised, there is a prima facie case for supposing that it encodes androcentric attitudes in an androcentric society. If so, then language itself is complicit in the oppression of women, and the business of a feminist linguistics is two-fold: to ascertain, by empirical investigations, just how far English usage discriminates against women, and to explain why language is much more of a prison-house for women than it is for men. The latter distinction is important. For after all, there is a long-standing philosophical tradition that language is a duplicitous medium, and that each of us – whatever our sex – is trapped inside the language we speak, such that (in Wittgenstein's aphorism) *'the limits of my language mean the limits of my world'*. Language, in other words, does not so much reflect reality as constitute it by structuring it according to its own categories. In Saussurean linguistics, for instance, this is believed to come about because the relationship between signifier and signified is always arbitrary: language is a self-referring system which interposes itself between ourselves and reality, denying us immediacy in the very act of mediation, offering us representations instead of presences, words instead of things. But here again the restrictions apply to both sexes equally. What a feminist linguistics must show is that language, in addition to being a prison in this general sense, is specifically a women's prison; and that linguistically speaking, women are doubly disadvantaged in being (as it were) prisoners of the male prisoners in the prison-house of language.

As social beings we have two principal encounters with language, and always in the same order: first when we are spoken of, and secondly when we ourselves learn to speak. In a non-feminist linguistics this raises the general problem of subjectivity and leads to the conclusion that, because language is already 'there' before we encounter it, and because we cannot hope to make ourselves understood unless we comply with its rules, we are in a sense 'spoken' by language, however much we may delude ourselves into believing that we control it when we learn to speak. Consequently, we do not have a prelinguistic subjectivity which we learn to 'express' in language; on the contrary, our subjectivity is produced for us in the language which constitutes our discourse ('I'm in words', Beckett's Unnamable comes to realise, 'made of words, others' words').[1] Folded into the ambiguities of 'subject' is not only the sense of freedom connoted by 'subjectivity' in liberal humanist discourse, but also the oppressiveness of 'subjection', and so Ann Oakley could hardly have chosen a better title for her book on the complex fate of being a woman than *Subject women* (London, 1981). In a specifically feminist linguistics, however, our two modes of entry into language constitute the grounds of two different though related enquiries. For to be spoken of in an androcentric society is to encounter verbal instances of sexism if you happen to be a woman; and to speak – or try to speak – is to experience difficulties in finding an appropriate speaking-position in an androcentric mode of discourse which designates men as the enunciators and relegates women to the position of the enounced.

If we concede that androcentrism is inscribed in language, the immediate question is, at what level? What kind of linguistics does feminism promote? Certainly not the kind proposed by Saussure when he dissociated individual utterances (*paroles*) from the linguistic system (*langue*) which makes such utterances possible, and did so in order to establish *langue* as the proper object of enquiry in a systemic linguistics. 'The phenomena feminists are concerned with have little to do with linguistic systems', Black and Coward point out. 'Language, as a system of phonological, syntactic, and logical structures and rules, is not inherently sexist or "man-made".'[2] So if the English language is felt to be sexist, it must be because of how we use it rather than because of what it is. And this means that the study of androcentrism in language comes within the competence of a sociolinguistics which is alert to the ways in which both masculine and feminine subject-positions are produced and reinforced in discourse. There is no prelinguistic and 'essential' masculinity which gets 'reflected' in language to the detriment of women, whose equally mythical femininity is consequently occluded and could be 'expressed' only by means of a totally different, female-specific language (although, as we shall see, such a project is entertained in certain types of feminist writing). But any society which organises itself on the basis of gender distinctions and uses language in order to mediate such distinctions will display homologically the same sorts of inequalities in its language as are revealed in a feminist analysis of its social practices. To shift the enquiry, therefore, from a systemic linguistics which investigates the nature of language to a sociolinguistics which treats language as a cultural phenomenon is an enabling manoeuvre with obvious polemical advantages. For in so far as cultural practices are variable they are mutable; and although we cannot transform our language habits overnight to get rid of what are felt to be undesirable characteristics, we have some chance of changing the ways in which men and women confer meaning on one another.

There is no shortage of testimonies to the effect that whether or not language was invented by men it serves their purposes much better than it serves women's. 'In speech with a man a woman is at a disadvantage', wrote Dorothy Richardson, 'because they speak different languages'; and seeing that a man 'will never speak nor understand' the language of a woman, 'she must therefore, stammeringly, speak his.'[3] The problem had been acknowledged already by Thomas Hardy's Bathsheba Everdene, who thought it 'difficult for a woman to define her feelings in language which is chiefly made by men to express theirs'.[4] What in a patriarchy goes euphemistically by the name of the mother tongue would be styled more accurately the 'father tongue' according to those who identify English as 'the oppressor's language' (Adrienne Rich) or 'Manglish' (Varda One).[5] Put in absolute terms, such claims sound exaggerated or even absurd. If men are so much at ease in language, why do male writers complain so often about compositional agonies and writer's block? And why has a long-standing rhetorical tradition designated fluency as a mere illusion created by painstaking craftsmanship? It is facile for a woman to attribute her difficulties in writing to the 'fact' that the medium itself is tailor-made for men. Not that the claim is in any sense a palliative for mediocrity in the case of Dorothy Richardson, who writes so well that it takes the form of an ironic humility reminiscent of those moments when Vladimir Nabokov apologises for his imperfect command of English. But if the proposition that women are not at home in language is phrased in social rather than absolute terms, it can be turned into a question worth trying to answer. 'How can female writers', asks Linda Gillman, 'work with a language produced by a social order in whose history they have played no part?'[6]

If you want to claim, however, as Gilbert and Gubar do, that writers like Fielding and Smollett 'implied that language itself was almost literally alien to the female tongue', you need better evidence than the presence of malapropisms in the speech of female characters created by those writers.[7] It is true that malapropisms are named after Sheridan's Mrs Malaprop in *The rivals* (1775); but as a comic device they were established in *A midsummer night's dream*, where Shakespeare makes them a characteristic feature of working-class speech (all the rude mechanicals are male). A much better place to start looking for evidence of the female self's alienation from language is in the pronoun system, and specifically in conventions governing first-person and third-person usage, the pronominal forms most immediately affected by the problematisation of speaking and of being spoken about. (Wariness of the first-person plural pronoun 'we' is also fairly common, but results from questioning the implications of critical consensus in some of the ways it is used − who is speaking, for instance, and for whom, in consensual statements like, 'We find a good deal of women's writing tediously prolix'? − rather than from any sense of maladjustment in the subject-position *vis-à-vis* language.) The crisis of subjectivity − the sense that 'I' denotes not a unified but a 'split' or divided self − was first articulated memorably by Arthur Rimbaud in a letter dated 13 May 1871: ' "I" is someone else' (*je est un autre*). Rimbaud's testimony weakens the common feminist claim that the crisis of identity is posed as a crisis of language for women only, and that whenever a man uses the first-person pronoun he produces that 'unified "I" ' which (in the words of Mary Jacobus) 'falls as a dominating phallic shadow across the male page'.[8] But if the linguistic expression of subjectivity is a problem for men as well as women, Cora Kaplan is right to suggest that complaints about it by women writers should be regarded 'as foregrounding the inherently unstable and split character of all human subjectivity' and not just the subjectivity of women.[9] The more common feminist view, however, is exemplified in Monique Wittig's statement that 'the "I" [*Je*] who writes is alien to her own writing at every word, because this "I" [*Je*] uses a language alien to her'.[10] The fractured ego is designated by a fractured signifier which, rendered typographically, turns *je* into *j/e*: the 'I' who finds herself without a phallus in the phallic domain of language could be written as '*j*'. Wittig says her fractured ł/e symbolises 'the exercise of a language which does not constitute m/e as a subject'.

Much of this becomes less enigmatic once you recognise that the wider frame of reference here is what anglophone critics refer to somewhat jocosely as French Freud.[11] This is the name given to

Jacques Lacan's revamping of Freud's theories of psychosexual development in infancy and early childhood. In Lacan's account, each of us starts life blissfully in a psychological state or 'order' called the Imaginary, but as our consciousness develops we find ourselves in the order of the Symbolic, which makes it possible for us to live in society, although at the price of exile from the Imaginary. In the Imaginary we experience what poets and mystics have called 'unity of being': convinced that we are part of our mother, we cannot distinguish between self and other, or imagine those alternatives to presence and possession which eventually we shall recognise as absence and lack. Unable to speak, the infant (Latin *infans*, 'speechless') is able to perceive itself only as it is perceived, and thus acquires that illusion of integral identity which obscures the reality of a division between self and (m)other. The shift from the Imaginary to the Symbolic is implicit in that Oedipal moment when the child is first aware of the father intervening between self and mother. Learning the meaning of absence and deprivation in the very act of registering this perception, the child acquires a place in which to store repression of what cannot now be had (the unconscious) and a symbolic system for articulating such absences and deprivations (language). The price to be paid for acquiring a speaking-position in the Symbolic, and mastery of the pronominal system which multiplies distinctions between self and other, is repression of desire for that lost unity with the mother. What symbolises for Lacan that separation and loss is the phallus which, despite Lacan's insistence that it is not to be identified with the penis, nevertheless appears to privilege the psychosexual development of boys at the expense of girls. For if the phallus is the prime signifier of the Symbolic and all it contains, including language, then domiciling themselves in the Symbolic is much more difficult for girls than for boys, who at least possess the organ which symbolically rules the Symbolic, and under whose aegis our phallocentric world is organised. Hence the attempts by Julia Kristeva and others to re-theorise feminine sexuality in such a way that entry into the Symbolic order of language is not mediated by the phallus and made subject to the law of the Father. Daughters might then feel at home in what would be truly a mother tongue, and Wittig's fractured *j/e* would heal. But in the meantime women will continue to be oppressed by the phallic regime of language, and incongruously obliged to 'become phallus' (in Kristeva's phrase) in order to speak the discourse of the community.[12]

Feminist discussions of third-person pronouns are much less

complicated, and focus on the consequences of using the word 'man' to denote not only members of the male sex but also human beings of both sexes, so that men are encouraged to think of themselves as representative of the human species. What gets called 'the generic masculine' or 'the preferential masculine' makes its presence felt pronominally in circumstances which appear to efface women altogether, for example in sentences such as, 'The reader will find he has to work things out for himself.' Once alerted to the problem, people eager to do something about it respond in a variety of ways. Poker-faced feminists silently substitute 'she' for 'he' in order to draw attention to the tacit gendering encoded in 'he': Ellen Moers does this throughout *Literary women* (London, 1978), at one stage rewriting Wordsworth's celebrated definition of a poet as 'a woman speaking to women' (p. 55). Some make the point less economically by spelling out every 'he' as 'he or she', and with deplorable consequences for their sentences, especially when every 'himself' has to become 'himself or herself'. Others rewrite 'he' as the unpronounceable 's/he' but find themselves stumped by 'himself'; people uninhibited by two centuries of prescriptive grammar replace 'he' by singular 'they', and then convert 'himself' into 'themselves'. The lunatic fringe proposes alternative common gender or epicene pronouns like 'E', 'hesh', 'po', 'tey', 've', 'xe', 'jhe', 'gen', 'thon', and 'per';[13] and experienced trouble-shooters simply rewrite such sentences with plural forms throughout ('Readers will find they have to work things out for themselves'). Exactly how the word 'man', which referred in Old English to people of either sex, came to be at once male-specific and supposedly not so, is still obscure. But in the wake of Ann Bodine's researches into the history of singular 'they', nobody can doubt that the rule governing the use of an allegedly sex-indefinite 'he' in connection with nouns denoting persons of either sex was made in the eighteenth century by prescriptive grammarians who simply ignored earlier and contemporary English usage, and who did so for reasons quite irrelevant to language study, but certainly conducive to the preservation of male supremacy, and to the replication of that supremacy in the symbolic order of language.[14] The most striking aspect of all this is that because the masculine is aligned so frequently with the universal, men are able to conceive of their own subjectivity as being non-gendered, and therefore wonder why feminists make such a fuss about gender. But because women are not aligned with the universal, they are much more inclined to see themselves as women than men are to see themselves as men. Consequently, as Black and Coward point out, 'one of the major political problems confronting feminism [is] the need to force men to recognize themselves as *men*'.[15]

It seems easier to find incontrovertible evidence of androcentric bias among those who talk about language than in language itself. After all, it was linguists who introduced the concept of gender into language study by classifying nouns as masculine, feminine or neuter; and although the gendering of language has provided generations of schoolteachers with opportunities for mild ribaldry (verbs conjugate, but nouns decline), there is no natural connection between the sex of something and the gender of the noun which designates it, as Mark Twain discovered before ridiculing 'The awful German language' for tolerating feminine buds and neuter leaves on masculine trees.[16] It was prosodists who decided to call rhymes ending on a stressed syllable 'masculine' and those ending on an unstressed one 'feminine'. And by designating consonants as male and vowels as female it has been possible since at least the seventeenth century − when Thomas Carew commented on the 'masculine' qualities of Donne's poetic language − to conceive of English as undeniably masculine in comparison with an 'effeminate' language like Italian.[17] Such attitudes turn up in textbooks. Ethel Strainchamps castigates Otto Jespersen for saying that English is 'the most positively and expressly masculine' of all the languages he knows because it has 'very little childish or feminine about it' − a collocation of adjectives which reveals his attitude to women more strikingly than his acuity as a linguist.[18]

There are various things worth looking at if you are interested in uncovering evidence of androcentric bias in linguistic usage. Take suffixes, for instance, like the '-ess' which turns 'actor' into 'actress' and 'poet' into 'poetess'. Here, because 'actor' and 'poet' happen to be words used of men, the creation of feminine agentives to describe the same activities done by women implies that women constitute at best some sort of special case and at worst an ersatz version of the real thing. Or take the case of naming: why have so many things pertaining to women been named in terms of their relation to men? In the case of personal names, for instance, why did an unmarried woman have to be styled 'Miss' and a married one 'Mrs' when both married and unmarried men were indistinguishably 'Mr'; and why did women have to lose their surnames on marrying, and sometimes even their first names (Mrs Humphry Ward)?[19] As for common nouns, why did the vagina have to be so called? Seeing that the Latin word means 'scabbard', the organ itself must have been named specifically for its secondary function in sheathing a penis. Throughout this book I have written 'men and women' but never 'women and men'. Does the order of the items in formulae like 'boys and girls' and 'men and women' exist so as to confirm the second sex in its secondariness; and if so, are sex-reversed formulae like 'bride and groom' and 'ladies and gentlemen' merely chivalrous exceptions which prove the rule? Formulae which give primacy to the male are defended sometimes on the grounds of euphony ('his or her' sounds better than 'her or his') or of rhythm ('men and women' is satisfyingly trochaic [-u-u] and 'ladies and gentlemen' even more satisfyingly dactylic [-uu-uu], and to tamper with their rhythms would be philistine). But to defend the formulae on aesthetic grounds leaves one at a loss to know what to do with exceptions which nevertheless still manage to give primacy to the male: as Casey Miller and Kate Swift point out, a taste for trochees is ignored in formulae like 'husbands and wives' and 'Adam and Eve'.[20] This is why the whole enterprise of tracking the oppressor's spoor in idiomatic usage needs to be conducted so scrupulously, for it is only too easy to amass examples which 'prove' that the English language either is or is not sexist in its usage. Take the case of collocations like Jespersen's 'childish or feminine', for instance. They are usually sexist, like Spenser's antifeminist line about 'fooles, women, and boys', and that proverbial couplet about 'A spaniel, a woman and a walnut-tree' ('the more they're beaten the better they be'); but a poem denouncing the 'rape / of a country / a girl / or an ape' turns up in a feminist anthology.[21] The conclusion pointed to by such anomalies is that language is not inherently sexist, but can be put to sexist uses. Even more significant, however, is the fact that stereotyped phrases and idioms which are disparaging to women can be presented in such a way as to make it appear that they are produced neutrally by inherent laws of language, or should be retained in the interests of purely aesthetic considerations, such as a pleasing rhythm or sequence of sounds. To probe here is to unmask the ideology of male dominance.

Understanding the language is one thing; changing it is another. If sexist usage outrages you, there are various ways of kicking against the pricks. One mode of intervention is reformist. It was first manifested early in the 1970s in publishers' instructions to writers, like the McGraw-Hill 'Guidelines for equal treatment of the sexes' and the Scott, Foresman 'Guidelines for improving the image of women in textbooks', and culminates in *The handbook of non-sexist writing*

(London, 1981) by Casey Miller and Kate Swift. Utilitarian and well intentioned, such publications teach people how to write discursive prose which will not be offensive to women. But like anything else they are capable of being misused and of giving excellent advice inadvertently on how to conceal one's sexism and feign feminist sympathies (racists who thought of negroes as niggers doubtless went on doing so long after it became politic to start calling them blacks). Other modes of reformism are not so systematised, and tend to be much less moderate in what they propose. In feminist discourse a new terminology has emerged for naming the hitherto unnamable: words like 'phallocracy' and 'gynocritics', for instance, which dismay the kind of reader who confuses technical language with jargon, but which gain acceptance because there is no other word to describe on the one hand a social order which is dominated by those whose privilege is grounded psychoanalytically in the Lacanian Symbolic, and on the other hand a specialised critical discourse for describing women as writers. New meanings get poured into old words: 'chauvinism' has nothing to do with patriotism any more; and 'no man's land', which acquired a lethal sense as the space between opposing trenches in the Great War, is now used of 'Adamless Edens' like those depicted in Gilman's *Herland* (1915) and Wittig's *Les guérillères* (1969).[22] Macho phrases undergo radical transformations when recycled as feminist irony ('watch your language, men').[23] Some of the neologisms remain nonce-words, such as 'testeria' (as the male version of 'hysteria') or 'phallustine'; others, like 'phallacy' (as in 'Freudian phallacy') inhabit a liminal zone between the serious and the farcical, partly because of deconstructionist incentives to free play. 'Mhysteria' and 'misstery' occur in feminist contexts, not in parodies: but is Pauline Bart being ironic when she says women should stop calling data 'hard' or 'soft' and start calling it 'wet' or 'dry'?[24] Theoretically, a neologism is justified if that is the only way of obtaining a non-sexist meaning; but difficulties are created by our unfamiliarity with the new words, and more so in creative than in critical writing. 'I'm not in retrosense', somebody remarks in Sally Miller Gearhart's novel *The wanderground* (1979), and we wonder what that would mean if she were. Or again: 'Alaka shifted to her lonth.' But a gloss follows immediately this time: 'that deep part of her kinaesthetic awareness that could take charge of her bodily movements in involuntary fashion'.[25]

Synchronic etymologising is rife in feminist discourse. 'We must learn to dis-spell the language of phallocracy', writes Daly, who sees

'male-functioning' in 'malfunctioning' and 'the/rapist' in 'thera-
pist'.[26] Even critics largely indifferent to deconstructionist revelry play
games with language, and readers of *The madwoman in the attic* (New
Haven, 1979) notice immediately that the derivation of 'pen' from
penna ('feather') does not tickle the fancy of Gilbert and Gubar nearly
so much as the ludic question, 'Is a pen a metaphorical penis?' (p. 3).
Dis-spelling (frequently indicated by the insertion of a slash:
'gyn/ecology') is a disruptive device which, together with syntactical
distortions, is intended to effect an intervention in the phallocratic
order of 'normal' English. By vandalising the language you publicise
the ways in which it oppresses those outside the phallocratic
dispensation. And by breeching the proprieties, you make an effort to
reclaim taboo words (as D. H. Lawrence tried to do in the case of those
once notorious four-letter words in *Lady Chatterley's lover*) in the
expectation of weakening the misogynistic power of 'bad' language by
using it descriptively rather than evaluatively: 'feminists have "tits"
and "cunts" ', writes Angela Carter, 'although we scrupulously excise
these terms, and, indeed, all sexual abuse, from the language of
imprecation'.[27] For as the Feminist Writers Workshop makes clear in
the subtitle of *An intelligent woman's guide to dirty words* (Chicago,
1973), the really dirty words are those 'reflecting sexist attitudes toward
women in patriarchal society'.

Moderate reformism and disruptive vandalism are both based on the
assumption that language is the dominant carrier of sexism in our
society, and that unless something is done about it the social problems
experienced by women will go on being transmitted from generation
to generation. Yet the compiling of feminist dictionaries and guidelines
to non-sexist usage goes very much against the spirit of descriptive
linguistics since Saussure, which has outlawed any kind of prescriptive
remodelling of language. Does this policy of non-intervention betray
a masculine obsession with 'objectivity' such as to make descriptive
linguistics complicit with the oppressive practices already encoded in
language? Whether or not language is or should be susceptible to
linguistic engineering is a moot point, given the poor success rate of
earlier attempts at purifying English of 'undesirable' elements. Usage
is notoriously counter-reformist, as we have begun to see. For if
married women continue to use the designation 'Mrs' instead of the
recommended 'Ms' (which indicates their sex without relating them to
a man in the process – and thus making them, in the Victorian sense,
'relative creatures'), then 'Ms' will come to serve the same purpose as

the currently discredited 'Miss'; and there is going to be no point in substituting 'chairperson' for 'chairman' if the only people who get referred to as chairpersons are women.[28] Usage is capable of making supposedly gender-free terms gender-specific, as is instanced in the tacit equation of 'adult' with 'male' in phrases like 'adult movies' and 'adult bookshops'. The problem for reformists is first to find the neutral words, and then to keep them neutral. Some despair of the possibility. 'Our language may be so infused with a tradition of inferred masculine referents', Erica Wise and Janet Rafferty report, 'that even the seemingly neutral words now in vogue ("person", "adult", etc.) may lead to masculine inference.'[29] This would be depressing news indeed if it were the case that words in common use always reflect the beliefs of those who use them. But clearly they do not. References to 'sunrise' and 'sunset' cannot be taken as evidence of a belief that the sun goes round the earth, any more than 'Christmas' denotes in common usage ('Where are you going for Christmas?') a commitment to the Church ritual celebrating the birth of Christ.

Underlying all this is an ancient debate about the way in which language relates to reality. The 'anomalist' view (which modern linguistics supports) is that because words are merely signs for things their relationship to reality is quite arbitrary: declaring war on the generic 'he' will therefore get you nowhere, for seeing that the cause of women's oppression lies outside language, the remedy cannot be found within it. The rival 'analogist' view, however, is that the order of language is the same as the order of things in general, such that changes in the one will effect 'isomorphic' changes in the other, and a revolution of the word will produce a revolution in the world.[30] Attempts to establish links between language and reality often rest on some direct or indirect reference to the so-called 'Sapir–Whorf hypothesis', which is commonly understood to mean that language determines thought. If that were true, then speakers of languages having the same linguistic features would manifest the same structures of thought, and it would be possible to predict what these could be. But Whorf in fact did not claim that there is a 'diagnostic' correspondence between language and thought; all he said was that we can *relate* certain linguistic features to certain patterns of thought. 'Whorf's linguistic observations do not count as evidence for cultural traits or "thought worlds" ', George L. Dillon concludes, 'but as illustrations of them in the domain of syntax and morphology.' Whorf's hypothesis is therefore an insecure base on which to construct the theory that

language is androcentric. 'From an analysis of the pronoun system of
a language', Dillon points out, 'we do not discover its attitude toward
women, nor can we prove that a culture is sexist after the English
speaking model by showing that it has an English-type pronominal
system.' The proper business of a Whorfian stylistics, he believes, is
not to pursue the unproven and probably unprovable hypothesis that
language determines thought, but to explain 'how social norms,
purposes and stereotypes are embedded in language'. That particular
Whorfian project should be welcomed by feminism, which has had a
good deal to say about stereotypical representations of women.[31]

ii

An obvious place to look for androcentric bias in a patriarchal culture
is in representations of women in literature and the visual arts,
including the media. One of the earliest forms of feminist criticism
focused accordingly on what was called 'images of women'. This was
partly because academic feminism was conceived of initially as some
sort of sociology in which literary texts could be used as evidence and
picked over to see what kind of role-models for women they supplied.
But it was also because 'thematics' (the study of literary themes) was
so well established in English studies that the thematising of women's
writing presented no methodological problems, however much
resistance there might have been to the incorporation of 'women's
literature' in academic syllabuses. In addition, Northrop Frye's
attempt to produce a grammar of literary archetypes conferred
academic respectability on the so-called myth criticism which derived
in part from Carl Jung's reconstruction of the archetypal imagery of
human experience.[32] So at a time when literary critics could still debate
whether the symbolic figures which turn up in literature are universal
'archetypes' or culture-specific 'phenotypes', Mary Ellmann published
a substantial essay in *Thinking about women* (New York, 1968) on
'Feminine stereotypes', which encouraged numerous researchers to
contribute detailed reports on the representation of women in a variety
of well-known authors in the expectation of transforming Ellmann's
sketch-map into an ordnance survey of the whole field.

To study images of women in a patriarchal society is to engage
inevitably in contradictory purposes. On the one hand, there is the
desire to unmask the oppressive nature of stereotypical representations
which, converted into role-models, offer an alarmingly limited view

of what a woman can expect of life; and on the other hand, there is the hope that by providing opportunities for thinking about women, and by comparing how they have been represented with how they ought to be, women's self-awareness will be heightened by a process known as consciousness-raising. This term originates in that social 'dialect' or sociolect called 'psychobabble' which emerged in California in the 1960s and was pilloried in *The serial* (New York, 1977), a satirical novel about Marin County by Cyra McFadden.[33] In a feminist context, 'consciousness-raising' came to signify a variety of related activities which are spelled out in Juliet Mitchell's definition: 'the process of transforming the hidden, individual fears of women into a shared awareness of the meaning of them as social problems, the release of anger, anxiety, the struggle of proclaiming the painful and transforming it into the political'.[34] What was not anticipated by those who planned academic courses on images of women was the dispiriting effect of sexist stereotypes on female students who had been encouraged to 'relate to' literature (psychobabble again) instead of studying it in the way that earlier generations had studied stock types of ancient comedy like the boastful soldier (*miles gloriosus*) or the revival of Theophrastan 'characters' in seventeenth-century English literature. 'One of the problems in teaching "The Images of Women in Literature" ', Mary Anne Ferguson reported, 'is fighting the depression which builds up as the essentially negative reflection is documented in story after story'; for as Sandra Lee Bartky puts it, 'feminist consciousness is consciousness of *victimization*'.[35] Patricia Meyer Spacks's students didn't want to talk about Doris Lessing's novel *Martha Quest* (1964) because its heroine 'reminded them too much of themselves. Recognizing her dilemmas, they feared her failure.'[36] The darker side of this experience is the suicidal despair recorded in one of the classics of current feminism, Kate Chopin's *The awakening* (1899), whose heroine awakens to consciousness on a beach while on holiday, and then swims out to sea and drowns herself. An alternative response to victimisation is the release of suppressed anger, which gets directed against men in general and sometimes against the nearest male: so Robin Rowland reports that it is not unheard of for students enrolled in women's studies 'to terminate their marriage while doing the course'.[37]

These somewhat sensational ramifications of what starts out as being no more controversial than any other pedagogic practice highlight the difficulty of trying to academicise material which many women feel cannot be handled 'objectively' because it touches too raw a nerve. Theoretically, of course, there is no reason why research into images of women in literature should not enrich our understanding of literary conventions by supplementing earlier studies of those reductionist practices which simplify human beings into types (or stereotypes) capable of being manipulated for a great variety of literary effects, ranging from the farcical to the tragic. And to a certain extent, this is what has happened. We now know in considerable detail the literary consequences of those man-made taxonomies which use binary categories in order to classify women as sensuous roses or virginal lilies, pedestalled goddesses or downtrodden slaves, Eves or Marys, Madonnas or Magdalenes, damned whores or God's police. As in archetypal criticism, the Bible and classical mythology are quarried as major deposits of types. Distinctions can be made between apparently archetypal images of the Great Mother (as exemplified, for instance, in Virginia Woolf's Mrs Ramsey in *To the lighthouse*) and obviously cultural stereotypes like the Great American Bitch as represented by Martha in Albee's *Who's afraid of Virginia Woolf?* (1962), whose function is to reinforce the sexist view that 'true happiness is based on True Womanhood, feminine subordination which supports male domination'.[38] The fact that cultural stereotypes attract more attention nowadays than archetypes is due to the success of marxist attacks on myth criticism as a reactionary discourse which hinders the transformation of society by pretending that a handful of allegedly transhistorical and immutable archetypes encode the only human experiences worth having. In some cases the *locus classicus* of a cultural stereotype can be pin-pointed exactly and its subsequent trajectory logged through novels and plays and poems, as in the case of 'the eternal feminine' in Goethe's *Faust* (1832). The title-image of Coventry Patmore's *The angel in the house* (1835) attracted renewed interest as an emblem of undesirable domestication after Virginia Woolf wrote that 'killing the Angel in the house [is] part of the occupation of a woman writer' ('Man must be pleased', Patmore wrote; 'but to please him / Is woman's pleasure').[39] Collectively, such images form a cultural shorthand which writers use in the confidence that every reader will recognise it.

The usual complaint from those who study images of women is that women tend to be conceived of only in terms of their relation to men, and the point is made as if this were surprising in a literature valued by a heterosexual society. Here is a typical instance:

Traditionally women's lives have been imagined in relation to men's lives, as the daughters, mothers, mistresses, wives of men. They have in consequence been imagined either in terms of a single role psychologically important to men (virgin, temptress, bitch, goddess) or in terms of their single social and biological function in male society (preparing for marriage, or married).[40]

In a rival 'images of men' style of enquiry directed at women's writing a good deal of this would be equally true if the terms were simply reversed: 'Traditionally men's lives have been imagined in relation to women's lives, as the sons, fathers, lovers or husbands of women.' Where an images-of-women approach gets its purchase is by being able to show that what is offensive in representations of women is not so much having them defined in relation to men as the fact that such relationships are often exploitative of women:

> A woman is a worthy thyng
> They do the washe and do the wrynge . . .
> A womane is a worthy wyght
> She serveth a man both daye and nyght.[41]

If Wilde was right and life imitates art, demeaning representations of women may have disastrous consequences by stabilising oppressive roles in memorable forms. Intervention is therefore seen as necessary to ensure that only 'suitable' representations are given prominence. Criticism gives up its pretence to describing the way things are and becomes unashamedly prescriptive, becoming as intolerant of sexism as Dickens' Mr Podsnap was of those topics which, if mentioned, would bring a blush to the cheeks of a young person. 'A literary work should provide *role-models*', Cheri Register insists, 'instill a positive sense of feminine identity by portraying women who are "self-actualizing, whose identities are not dependent on men".'[42] But what can you do with a text once you have exposed it? Reformation zealots had no qualms about destroying church ornaments and vestments which they saw as the corrupt artefacts of a corrupt religion; the Nazis destroyed art deemed decadent. But book-burning is hardly available as an option for feminists, and so any reformism which is predicated on the supposition that men can be shamed into changing their ways is jeopardised inevitably by the indifference or renewed aggression of impenitent sexists like Norman Mailer.[43] Whether acknowledged or not, censorship is inevitable in the compiling of a feminist syllabus, especially if one of the criteria for selection is that the work should instil a positive sense of feminine identity. The question Phyllis Franklin asked herself when considering Sophocles' *Antigone* as a possible set-text was not whether it is regarded as a good or even a historically important play but 'whether it would be a good thing for . . . students to simply accept Antigone as a role model' (Antigone, it will be recalled, is self-sacrificing, 'and surely we have had enough of that').[44] This sounds ominously like ' "the brownie-point approach" to women's history' mocked by Marilyn B. Arthur: 'if Medea gets three points for asserting herself and exacting revenge from Jason, then she loses one for killing her children, forfeits another for using deceit and trickery, another for relying on her grandfather to get her out of the mess, and ends up with a score of zero'.[45] Somehow the canonical texts of an ideal images-of-women course are expected to constitute a kind of conduct book, offering women readers what Elaine Showalter calls 'authentic and primary identities' in place of all those 'secondary and artificial images women receive from a male chauvinist society'.[46]

Although promoted for admirable reasons, images-of-women criticism is bedevilled by various problems, among which are repetitiousness and a passion for confirmation at any cost. A charitable view would be that repetition is inevitable, given the history and ubiquity of man's inhumanity to woman, and the tendency of male writers by and large to overlook the exploitative nature of men's dealings with women; but boredom sets in quickly with the *déjà-lu*, and the consequences can be counterproductive. It may well be argued that to complete the record of iniquities is imperative, lest we forget. But anybody intending to engage in this task ought to bear in mind Lillian Robinson's caveat about 'the limitations of a feminist criticism that does no more than expose sexism in one work of literature after another'.[47] It certainly takes more than a little effort to persevere with a mode of enquiry whose conclusions are so evidently foregone. The objection that images-of-women criticism can be very boring to read is vulnerable, however, to the counter-charge that it was never intended to be entertaining, and that in any case it is no more boring than most criticism, the reading of which is the price you pay if you choose to study literature. Much more pertinent is the semiotic objection that an images-of-women approach treats 'woman' as a pre-given entity whose unchanging and transhistorical essence − 'the eternal feminine' − gets represented (or more often misrepresented) in various texts at various times. The semiotic view is that 'woman' is never a given in that sense, but is always the product of an ideological construction. And this is why more recent work in this area prefers to speak of 'representation' as a process rather than of 'images' as products. Furthermore, the production of 'woman' in discourse is not limited to those discourses in which women are the sole subject, but on the contrary traverses many different discourses — medical, legal, biological, psychoanalytic and so on — with the result that 'woman' is a sort of 'intertext' inscribed by these different discourses. The proper study of 'woman' is consequently a trans-disciplinary venture, and certainly not something which literary critics can be presumed to know all about before turning to the texts which claim to represent her.

A good deal depends, therefore, on which representations get chosen for their representativeness. In images-of-women criticism we are given the impression that they have somehow selected themselves, with a little help from a feminist ideology which classifies some images as desirable and others as not. For example, if it is agreed that Victorian patriarchal attitudes were particularly hard on women, all you have to do is select an image which supports that view, and then track its manifestations through various texts. The more manifestations you can trace, the more dominant it appears to be. This is what seems to have happened in the case of that emblem of selfless love, the angel in the house, the sexual politics of which is that Victorian men were happy to idealise women provided they stayed in their proper sphere — the home — and posed no threat to men in the world at large. The problem is then to decide what to do with other Victorian representations of women which don't fit the angelic stereotype, specifically those 'demonic' representations (produced by both male and female writers) which Nina Auerbach examines, and which subvert what are taken to be officially sanctioned models of Victorian womanhood.[48] These rival images of women, which constitute 'a myth crowning a disobedient woman in her many guises as heir of the ages and demonic savior of the race', are embedded in a social mythology by means of which Victorians tried to explain themselves to one another. The function of such myths, as Claude Lévi-Strauss demonstrated in *Mythologiques* (Paris, 1964–71), is to embody contradictions in human experience, contradictions which a marxist style of analysis is particularly adept at locating and unravelling. If a society believes that its women both are and are not angelic, then its representations of them will be ambivalent. Little is to be gained, therefore, by trying to prove that the demonic images constitute a suppressed feminist alternative to patriarchy's angels; for as Auerbach notes, 'these subversive paradigms are only incidentally feminist'. And the conclusion pointed to by her case-study would seem to be that one of the ways in which an images-of-women style of criticism might renew itself is by deconstructing the premises on which it was originally based, and taking account of what gets excluded in the pursuit of allegedly dominant modes of representation.

If you are convinced that everything is politics, then how women are represented in literature is only one of the things you might want to look at closely if your intention is to uncover sexism in literary studies. How certain ways of doing things come to have the status of literary conventions is another site worth investigating. Like the study of character stereotypes, this too was a well-established and apparently apolitical enterprise in literary studies, especially after Ernst Robert Curtius had traced with inimitable authority the *topoi* or commonplaces which got transmitted from generation to generation under the influence of a rhetorical tradition which advised orators to collect commonplaces so that they would never be at a loss for examples when speaking in public.[49] These *topoi* enter literature as conventional images like the *theatrum mundi*, which Shakespeare remembered when writing that soliloquy in *As you like it* which begins, 'All the world's a stage' (II vii). As such they form part of any writer's repertoire, and the aim of scholarship is to reassemble these scattered commonplaces with a view to contextualising any instance of any one of them. Seeing that little attention if any is paid to the question of why some things rather than others achieve conventional status, the business of political criticism is to ask the politicising question: whose interests do these conventions serve? To Marcia R. Lieberman, a literary convention is never 'purely' that but rather 'the most subtle, pervasive level at which sexism affects literature'.[50] Viewed apolitically, the device of ending stage comedies with a marriage is an economical way of tying up loose narrative ends; but as a device for bringing women legally under the control of men, its popularity as a dramaturgical device is not insignificant in a patriarchal society. Similarly, the 'two suitor' convention in fiction (described by Jean E. Kennard), which obliges the heroine to choose between two men – one of whom may be an exciting Mr Wrong, and the other a staid Mr Right – operates the ideology that every woman needs a husband, and couldn't possibly lead a fulfilling life either alone or with another woman.[51] The gendering of this novelistic convention is clear by comparison with the parallel convention for male characters, the Choice of Hercules between a life of Virtue and a life of Vice. For female characters, 'choice' does not mean choosing a life-style but choosing a husband. But the restrictive nature of that ideological requirement is masked by a displacement of interest from the primary question – 'Why marry at all?' – to a subsequent one: 'How do I recognise Mr Right?' What are inscribed in our society as cultural practices are reaffirmed as literary conventions, and give the illusion of justifying their existence by imitating life. But 'life' itself, of course, is never pre-given and unconstructed, but always and already culturally coded, so that what we witness at those times when art appears to be uncannily like life is the momentary congruence of one set of codes with another.

If you wanted to investigate the sexual politics of *topoi* in something closer to Curtius' sense, then a good place to begin would be with the imagery in those marriage-poems which constitute a minor genre known as the epithalamy. There we encounter the 'elm and vine' *topos*, which is used so frequently that it functions like a generic marker to remind us what sort of poem we are reading. Given the traditional link between marriage and propagation, the *topos* represents the two sexes as mutually complementary, with the stronger husband/elm supporting the weaker wife/vine while she produces the fruits of her womb. But the sweet reasonableness of it all belies a sexual politics which is immediately oppressive to any woman who doesn't see herself as a vine or trust her elm to remain supportive. And part of that tacit politics – neutralised by the status of this *topos* in literary history as a conventional ornament in epithalamies – was brought out into the open on 28 July 1837, when the Council of Congregational Ministers of Massachusetts issued their pastoral letter denouncing Angelina Grimké for her unseemly behaviour in speaking publically against slavery: 'If the vine, whose strength and beauty is to lean upon the trellis-work, and half conceal its clusters, thinks to assume the independence and the overshadowing nature of the elm, it will not only cease to bear fruit, but fall in shame and dishonor into the dust.'[52] This nineteenth-century revival of an ancient epithalamic image in order to curb an unruly woman cannot fail to have a retroactive influence on our understanding of earlier instances of it, which legitimate as 'natural' a construction of male–female relationships which is in fact not natural at all but the product of 'culture' (specifically viticulture, in so far as vines don't grow naturally on elms, but used to be trained to do so by vine-growers).

The conventions of criticism are just as susceptible to this type of gender-analysis as the conventions of literature, as Marilyn R. Farwell demonstrates in her scrutiny of the theory that poets use masks or *personae* when they write, and do so in order to distance themselves from their subject-matter and thus create the conditions in which art rather than confession becomes possible. *Persona*-theory was introduced into criticism earlier this century as an antidote to crudely biographical attempts at reconstructing the private lives of poets from their poems; it seemed a plausible enough manoeuvre, given that T. S. Eliot had proclaimed the impersonality of great poetry, and Ezra Pound had collected his shorter poems under the title *Personae* (1926). To Farwell, however, to consider *persona*-theory solely in the context of biographism is to obscure its gender-bias. 'The theory of the persona incorporates the masculine virtues of separation and objectivity', she claims, and it therefore discredits 'the female inclination to relate to and to identify with reality.'[53] What is being objected to here is the unsuitability of a *persona*-based style of criticism when dealing with any kind of poetry written by women, and especially the new women's poetry evoked by Muriel Rukeyser's rallying cry, 'No more masks!'[54] 'A feminist criticism', Farwell believes, 'will have to provide a critical apparatus to allow the values of identity and relationship to be part of the poetic voice.'[55]

Missing from political accounts of literary conventions is a satisfactory explanation of why so many writers find it liberating to use them. Consider, for example, the Petrarchan convention of unrequited love, which occupied European writers for some three hundred years. In a macho critique, Petrarchism is a bore if not an insult to the virile, because for every girl who turns down a sexual proposition there is another one who doesn't, which means that any man who suffers sexual deprivation is a wimp; and in a feminist critique, Petrarchism is offensive because in placing women on a pedestal it represents them merely as unspeaking and unfeeling objects of men's desires. Neither view takes account of what must have been an important reason for the durability of this particular convention: namely that the literary imagination is stimulated far more productively by sexual frustration than by gratified desire, and that the autonomy of Petrarchism as a convention opened up the possibility of comic as well as serious literary treatments of love, as is evidenced by the intertwining of Petrarchan with anti-Petrarchan modes throughout the history of this literary fashion. Similarly, when Pierre Fauchery reports that 'in the eighteenth century, the myths of a feminine destiny as created by men are for the most part adopted as is by women novelists,'[56] we have to entertain the possibility that the reason for this was that such myths made it easier to write the kind of novels people wanted to read — however tempting it might be to see here yet another instance of the domination of women by patriarchal modes of thought encoded in seemingly gender-free conventions.

The rider to Muriel Rukeyser's 'No more masks!' is 'No more mythologies!' This is taken sometimes as meaning that a literature produced by and for women will be free of myth altogether; but that would be impossible. Every act of demythologising involves a corresponding act of remythologising, and even if large numbers of people were to believe in 'the myth of mythlessness' the outcome would be a body of writing which, far from being myth-free, would merely exemplify 'the mythology of no more mythologies'. (The same is true of course of masks: what a writer reveals when she removes her mask is not her face but the mask of masklessness.) 'No more mythologies' makes better sense if interpreted to mean 'No more patriarchal mythologies', for it is these which trick women into putting up with conditions which they would otherwise find intolerable. 'Romantic love' is one such myth which traps heterosexual young women into underachieving at school and sacrificing careers of their own in the expectation that the most important thing in their lives is to marry the right man and live with him happily ever after. To Shulamith Firestone, romantic love is consequently 'the pivot of women's oppression',[57] because it induces women to submit willingly to their own subjection, and survives even the most corrosive of attacks, such as the publicity given to divorce statistics and to the testimonies of various women who eventually saw through it all, but too late. 'Motherhood' is another such myth which deflects attention from what Françoise Basch calls 'the calvary of pregnancy' by making it out that giving birth to a child is always a supremely fulfilling and ennobling experience, despite the fact that even the normally reticent Queen Victoria confessed to feeling 'like a cow or a dog at such moments'.[58] As the patriarchy needs sons in order to perpetuate itself, and the principal source of sons is still women, 'motherhood' comes to be construed as the ultimate destiny of essential womanhood. It thus joins those other repressive mythologies which collaborate in the subordination-by-domestication of women, and which Charlotte Perkins Gilman labelled 'the Kaiser's four K's − Kuchen, Kinder, Kirche, Kleider' (cooking, children, church and clothes).[59]

Fairy-tales are among the cultural forms which help consolidate this belief that the best thing which can happen to a girl (the passive construction is significant here) is to fall in love, get married and have lots of children. To Karen E. Rowe, 'fairy tales are not just entertaining fantasies, but powerful transmitters of romantic myths which encourage women to internalize only aspirations deemed appropriate to [their] "real" sexual functions within a patriarchy'; to Marcia R. Lieberman they are 'training manuals for girls' which 'serve to acculturate women to traditional roles'.[60] What does a girl learn from them? Principally that she is by nature a passive creature, like the princess who waits patiently on top of the Glass Hill for the first man to climb it. She learns also that she is symbolically dead (either asleep like Sleeping Beauty or incarcerated like Rapunzel) until brought to life by the man who will be the man in her life. Submissive and helpless, she must expect to drift from one kind of dependency to another without ever exercising her autonomy, her consciousness of which has never been raised. She should hope she is beautiful because beauty ranks as worthiness in androcentric scales of value. She should avoid being an ugly sister, cruel stepmother, hag or witch, for men find all such women sexually undesirable. Fairy-tales fragment the continuities of female life into discontinuous states, with the result that young princesses tend to regard hags and witches as belonging to a different species rather than as possible versions of themselves in a few years' time. Fairy-tales focus on the princess because men prefer younger women: hence the shock when Anne Sexton rewrites some of *Grimm's fairy tales* from the point of view of 'a middle-aged witch, me'.[61] In a realm of magical goings-on, the principal enchantment for a girl is courtship, which leads her to suppose that the best way of perpetuating enchantment is by marrying the enchanter and living with him happily ever after. At that point she encounters reality.

   To go on in this vein about a collection of stories which many people would never dream of taking seriously — because they're 'only fairy stories' — might be considered somewhat excessive, especially as girls hardly need preternatural acuteness nowadays to discover that 'you gotta kiss a lotta frogs before you find Prince Charming'.[62] When it is suggested (by Rowe, for instance) that women need a completely new set of fairy-tales — perhaps along the lines of Alison Lurie's *Clever Gretchen and other forgotten folktales* (New York, 1980) — because those we have inherited from the nineteenth century are too reactionary by feminist standards, we seem to encounter a familiar impulse to censorship: the conviction that other people need protection against bad influences which appear to have had no irremediable effects upon oneself. Besides, it might be argued, the dominance of television as a medium for beguiling children has altered the cultural conditions which formerly sustained the telling or reading of fairy-tales. The transmission of them from generation to generation is likely to become even more of a minority activity, therefore, when children who were themselves reared on television programmes and video-games grow up and have children of their own to entertain. How 'typical' are the fairy-tales deemed typical in feminist modes of enquiry, with their emphasis on 'Sleeping Beauty', 'Cinderella', 'The Frog Prince' and a few others? If their effect on girls is so very pernicious, why is it that most of the informants used by the Grimms when collecting fairy-tales were women? If they are old-wives' tales, don't they therefore constitute some sort of women's literature? Hasn't Margaret Atwood testified, in naming the complete *Grimm's fairy tales* (New York, 1944) as the book she has re-read most frequently, 'that women in these stories are not passive zombies'?[63] In a larger perspective, feminist anxiety about the malign influence of fairy-tales on young girls is merely the most recent of a series of significant 'moments' in the history of their reception, such as when they were nationalised as archetypally Germanic tales fit for young Nazis, or psychologised as embodying the passage rites to sexual maturity in girls as well as boys, which is how Bruno Bettelheim reads them in *The uses of enchantment* (New York, 1976). 'What woman must learn to assume', writes Carolyn G. Heilbrun, with Bettelheim's book in mind, 'is that she is not confined to the role of the princess; that the hero, who wakens Sleeping Beauty with a kiss, is that part of herself that awakens conventional girlhood to the possibility of life and action.'[64]

A strong defence of the feminist position against such erosions of it is to argue that the uncertain future of fairy-tales as a text designed specifically to be read is neither here nor there, because what is at issue is the dissemination of fairy-tale attitudes through a great variety of cultural forms and practices, ranging from children's television programmes to enormously popular romances written for women. What is technically a fairy-tale (in the literary-critical sense) is merely the model for various types of fairy-tale romance produced in a variety of media and aimed at women of all ages. Everything depends, therefore, on whether you think people are influenced by what they read, and if so, what to do about it, especially if some of the things they read are fairy-tale romances which cripple women intellectually and emotionally. The first question is the one faced traditionally by any guardian of the social mores, who has to decide whether to follow

Plato and ban certain books from the republic because of their corrupting influences, or whether to tolerate them as Aristotle tolerated tragedy (that is, as a safety valve for desires which need to be expressed), and look upon fairy-tales and fairy-tale romances as necessary fodder for a fantasy-life which is no more harmful than day-dreaming if channelled into socially acceptable forms.

Radical feminists, in their dealings with fairy-tales, find themselves on account of their reformist tendencies in the position of Plato's censor, and somewhat embarrassingly aligned with reactionaries who would like to see a great many things banned, radical feminism among them. The paradoxes of this position are felt most keenly in the area of children's books, the writing of which (like the writing of women's romances) is predominantly a female occupation. There is much debate on whether a literature designed specifically for children should prepare them for the sexism of everyday life or shelter them from it. 'Some people think it wrong to portray for children the world as it is or was', argues Jill Paton Walsh, an experienced writer of children's fiction who doesn't agree with 'sanitising reality in order to change it'.[65] Once again, a laudable intention results in an undesirable effect. For the desire to combat sex-role stereotyping by eliminating representations of it from the earliest texts children read − and doing so with the full cooperation of publishers who don't want their investments threatened as a result of having their books blacklisted by feminist organisations − results in practices in which adverse critics detect the illiberality of the liberated. Opinions therefore vary as to whether feminist reformism is a sinister or merely ridiculous phenomenon. It will seem ridiculous if it reminds you (as it reminds Gillian Avery) of Sarah Trimmer's *The guardian of education* (1802–4), which scanned children's books for evidence of atheism and Jacobinism; but it will seem rather more sinister if you take the point of Carole Ferrier's comparison with the Stalinist promotion in the 1930s of 'socialist realism', and the concomitant hostility towards any work which did not reproduce the approved ideology.[66] Either way, children are powerless to prevent books written especially for them from being 'improved' or 'corrupted' by ideological interventions which are always said to be made in the best interests of children.

iii

Many of the traditionally sanctioned ways of representing women in literature appear to be not only antifeminist but also anti-female, and to be powered by a loathing of women which sees them as the root of all evil. In the pagan tradition it was Pandora who opened the box from which all the world's evils emerged; and in the Christian tradition, paradise was lost because Adam was tempted by Eve, that *Eva* whose very name is an anagram of *vae* ('woe'), and is the source of a disparaging etymology preserved in the seventeenth-century spelling of 'woman' as 'woeman'. What is implicitly misogynistic in the Old Testament account of the Fall of Man becomes explicitly so in the New Testament, where St Paul makes it clear that women are inferior creatures which fallen man is obliged to put up with for procreative purposes but whose influence on him should be negligible. To sustain such a view against the grain of sexual desire, it was necessary for men to read the Bible in a peculiarly blinkered way. For that cornucopian text is not uniformly hostile to women, and the perfect man who occupies its ideological centre was certainly no misogynist, despite the absence of a token woman among the apostles. As the Elizabethan poet Emilia Lanier was to point out, Jesus Christ was 'begotten of a woman, borne of a woman, nourished of a woman, obedient to a woman . . . healed women, pardoned women, comforted women'.[67] So just as Marx felt he wasn't really a marxist, Jesus may have had difficulty recognising himself as an early Christian. 'The foundations of early Christian misogyny − its guilt about sex, its insistence on female subjection, its dread of female seduction − are all in St Paul's epistles', writes Katharine M. Rogers in her history of misogyny in literature.[68] The legacy was consolidated by the so-called 'Fathers' of the early Church, like Tertullian, who thought a woman was not only 'the gateway of the devil' but also 'a temple built over a sewer'.[69] And this patristic tradition, grounded in an ascetic style of life which construed sexual desires as diabolical temptations imperilling the soul, was transmitted through monastic writings and sermons in the medieval period, and constituted the doctrinal orthodoxy with which Chaucer plays so skilfully when taking up misogynistic themes in *The Canterbury tales*, notably in the prologue to 'The wife of Bath's tale', where antifeminist quotations from St Jerome are defused ironically in the context of marital banter.

Male aggression against the female is capable of being displaced either into language, where it comes out as vituperation, or into art-forms, where it reproduces women as objects of sadistic humiliation, especially in pornography; undisplaced, it results in the rape and murder of women, often perpetrated with unspeakable elaborations. The persistent strain of misogyny in literature is therefore a matter of concern to anybody who views symbolic aggression as existing in the same continuum as acts of physical violence. There is no shortage of explanations as to why men behave so aggressively towards women, and many of these are grounded in the theory that men abuse women to disguise the fact that they fear them in some way. So if a man feels sexually inadequate, for instance, he may disguise his fear of sexually mature women as disgust at their 'insatiability', and invent 'nymphomania' as a female sexual disorder, or imitate Juvenal's sixth satire against the lusts of Roman matrons. Similarly, male sexual guilt − a man's fear that his own sexual desires are abnormal − may result in the construction of women as 'temptresses' whose 'degrading' behaviour needs to be punished. Inside any closely knit male-supremacist organisation, women are likely to be conceived of as matter out of place, which is an anthropological definition of dirt. An insecure male dominated by his mother will try to ensure that 'threatening' women meet their come-uppance. And above all there is the male fear of woman as the unknown, 'the deepest fear', as Otto Weininger called it, 'which is the fear of unconsciousness, the alluring abyss of annihilation'.[70] The only thing women are guilty of in these cases is failing to comply with male specifications of what they ought to be.

Literary works indubitably contain features which can only be labelled misogynistic. What is in question is why they are there, especially in periods not dominated (as the early nineteenth century was) by an expressivist view of writing as an outpouring of the writer's personal opinions. In earlier periods, when the connection between writing and rhetoric was stronger, the kind of writing which gets called literature nowadays was thought of as belonging to the 'epideictic' branch of rhetoric, the rhetoric of display, and capable of being explained in terms of 'praise' and 'dispraise'. A competent writer was one who knew how to produce poems in praise of his mistress' eyebrows (or whatever) for amatory purposes, as well as poems dispraising her for comic or satirical purposes. So John Donne wrote 'The extasie' in praise of women and 'Loves alchymie' dispraising them; what he 'really' thought about women is not deducible from these poems, and in any case would not be an issue in an assessment of his performance in either genre, which would involve taking account of his disposition of the materials appropriate to each kind of poem.

As rhetoricians, writers were encouraged to collect *exempla* (morally significant 'examples') from history, the Bible and classical mythology. Dispraisers drew attention to the goings-on of such figures as Clytemnestra, the Queen of Sheba, Cleopatra, Hippolyta, Judith and so forth. 'Oddly enough', Ruth Kelso comments, 'most of these examples appeared in the list for defense also.'[71] Rogers notes that a poem by John Lydgate called 'Examples against women', written in the fifteenth century, 'appears to be a literary exercise rather than an arraignment', and concedes that 'misogyny was a popular theme for rhetorical exercises'.[72] If so, then literary texts produced under the influence of this rhetorical tradition cannot be considered indisputable evidence of misogyny, since the ability to display misogynistic arguments for amusing or instructive purposes is not the same as 'expressing' misogynistic sentiments. Such arguments may well have been intended to be instructive in the way that Donne said his paradoxes were: 'if they make you to find better reasons against them, they do their office'.[73] Their purpose, in other words, was not to solicit belief, but by their very outrageousness to provoke dissent. As such, they had the same function as the 'evidence' of female inferiority against which feminist arguments are rehearsed in book 3 of Castiglione's influential *Book of the courtier* (1528), or as the statement 'Woman is not a human being', which turns up as a joke in various Renaissance texts, although always, Ian Maclean points out, 'the effect of the joke is to reinforce the contrary proposition: woman is a human being'.[74]

That may seem a risky way of going about things, given the fact that people sometimes mask aggression by claiming to be 'only joking'; and it is true that, whatever the justification in terms of rhetorical theory, a text which stockpiles misogynistic materials for any reason whatsoever can still be thought of as perpetuating misogyny and encouraging misogynistic interpretations. Nevertheless, it is important to contextualise writing which can be made to seem highly offensive if read out of context. Recent studies of medieval *fabliaux*, for instance, reveal that a text which contains misogynistic elements is not necessarily contained by them.[75] Women are certainly depicted in the *fabliaux* as adulterous and deceitful by nature, and in that respect exemplify many of the shortcomings catalogued by Andreas Capellanus in his *Remedium amoris*; but the women thus depicted are so quick-witted and resourceful as to make fools of most of the men they encounter – husbands especially – and are not presented in such a way as to invite disapproval of their behaviour. If a satirist conceives of the whole world as a Ship of Fools, women passengers can't expect to receive preferential treatment, and it becomes difficult to draw the demarcation lines between misogyny in particular and that more generalised misanthropy which characterises satirical writing. So it is important to take account of the conditions in which misogynistic writing appears. The fact that John Fletcher could write both a taming-of-the-shrew play (*Rule a wife and have a wife*, 1624) and an anti-taming-of-the-shrew play (*The woman's prize*, 1611) demonstrates not only the rhetorical versatility of writers in this period but also a sense of the market-value of a controversial subject. Carroll Camden cites instances of feminist and antifeminist tracts being written by the same person and printed by the same publisher.[76] If men appear to have spent more time abusing women than women men (which is what the textual evidence suggests), this is not because misandry is a more rare phenomenon than misogyny, but because for several centuries most printed books were written by men. 'If wommen hadde writen stories', Chaucer's wife of Bath points out, 'They wolde han writen of men moore wikkednesse / Than al the mark of Adam may redresse'[77] – to which one can only add that feminist writing published during the last fifteen years or so has been doing what it can to ensure that misandry will eventually be as well represented in print as misogyny now is.

Among the many forms taken by misogyny, pornography is believed to be particularly odious, and something which women should want to have nothing to do with at all, except to campaign for its abolition. Yet the most eloquent defence of pornographic writing is by Susan Sontag, who treats it as a literary genre which, like science fiction, encompasses a disproportionate amount of trash, but cannot be excluded automatically from the category of the literary on account of its subject matter alone ('mere' pornography).[78] To Sontag, just as we can speak of a 'visionary imagination' when discussing Dante or Blake, so we should speak of a 'pornographic imagination' in connection with classics like Pierre Louÿs' *Trois filles et leur mère* (1950), Georges Bataille's *Histoire de l'oeil* (1928) and *Madame Edwarda* (1937), and a couple of pseudonymous works, *Story of O* (1954) by 'Pauline Réage', and *The image* (1956) by 'Jean de Berg'. A common response to such works is to treat them as psychopathological in origin and as having undesirable social consequences, especially for women; but Sontag will have none of that, arguing instead that what makes these particular books classics is their original and fearless exploration of 'extreme forms of consciousness that transcend social personality or psychological individuality'. No matter how much we try to tame it, 'sexuality remains one of the demonic forces in human consciousness'. The pornographic imagination is valuable because it articulates fantasies we all entertain from time to time but refuse to acknowledge: 'Everyone has felt (at least in fantasy) the erotic glamour of physical cruelty and an erotic lure in things that are vile and repulsive.' Vicariously, we are able to experience in pornography desires which are socially unacceptable but which are part of the spectrum of sexuality. On the far side of those desires is the frightening revelation 'that what pornography is really about, ultimately, isn't sex but death'. And if we ask why it is that most pornography is so ludicrously inadequate, the answer lies in 'the traumatic failure of modern capitalist society to provide authentic outlets for the personal human flair for high-temperature visionary obsessions'. Instead of trying to stamp out pornography, therefore, we should be upgrading the quality of it, because we deserve something better than the crude rubbish currently available.

You would scarcely guess from this presentation of pornography as a much-misunderstood medium for exploring the limits of the erotic imagination that Sontag and (say) Andrea Dworkin have been reading the same book when they write about *Story of O*. To Dworkin, *Story of O* cannot be a classic of anything except woman-hating, because it chronicles relentlessly the inevitable consequences of the sado-masochistic construction of woman as victim. It construes male–female as a master–slave relationship, and presents us with a heroine who is 'fucked, sucked, raped, whipped, humiliated, and tortured on a regular and continuing basis' until she eventually kills herself, having been compelled to realise that the 'o' of each of her bodily orifices is a zero which symbolises her nothingness in a man's world.[79] What is called 'sex' in our society ought to be called therefore by its proper name, which is 'sexism'; and the only thing to be said in favour of pornography is that it does indeed spell out the connection between sex and violence which is at the heart of that peculiarly masculine view of sexuality which fails to recognise itself as male-specific. By reinforcing the macho myth that every woman secretly wants to be raped,[80] pornography has pernicious social consequences which cannot be glossed over by intellectualising it in the way that Sontag does. Slogans like Beverly LaBelle's 'Pornography is the propaganda of misogyny' and Robin Morgan's 'Pornography is the theory, and rape the practice' summarise the feminist opposition which gets most publicity.[81] And in quieter moments, when anger is muted as pathos, Susan Griffin can lament that 'we have mistaken eros for pornography'.[82] The latter distinction would be crucial to the debate if it were not so controversial, because then it would be possible to argue, as Gloria Steinem does, that 'erotica is about sexuality, but pornography is about power and sex-as-weapon'; but the neatness of this demarcation of interests does not impress people who find the distinction more formal than substantial, and who would agree with Angela Carter that erotica is simply 'the pornography of the elite'.[83]

What seems to have happened is that the object addressed as pornography in feminist discourse has changed its status since the 1960s. In the liberation movements out of which feminism grew, pornography was one of the insignia by means of which counter-cultural men and women (who wanted to 'make love, not war') dissociated themselves from the older generation which had got America into a cold war with Russia and a real war in Vietnam. In that context, the cult of pornography was liberating, as indeed it still was for Angela Carter in 1979 when she advised women to read the most notorious of the classic pornographers, the Marquis de Sade, because he encourages women to break with the model of sexual passivity imposed upon them patriarchally, 'to fuck their way into history and, in doing so, change it'.[84] Even the non-radical liberals of the 1960s defended the right of everybody to read books hitherto banned (although written by such respected authors as D. H. Lawrence and Henry Miller) on account of their sexual explicitness. One by one those books were put on trial and acquitted. But it was clear that the feminist case levelled at *Lady Chatterley's lover* and *Tropic of Capricorn* by Kate Millett in 1970 was even more pertinent if directed against what Sontag would call pornographic trash. What had inhibited the publication of pornography for popular consumption was a legal definition of obscenity which turned out to be so untenable that the Williams Committee recommended dropping the criterion altogether. If that were to happen, no book — however 'obscene' — could be judged obscene.

Perhaps this is why feminists have devoted less attention recently to the representation of women in pornographic books than in films, television and advertising, thus effecting a redefinition of pornography as rather a 'showing' than a 'writing' (*porne* 'prostitute', *grapho* 'write'). It is not a question nowadays of what we can say, but of what we can see, and so the debate about pornography is no longer (as it was in the 1960s) a literary critical issue: the terrain of the dispute is now media studies and film criticism. Much of what goes on there, however, is clearly relevant to an understanding of literary critical attitudes to pornography. For the myth of the 'one undifferentiated male viewer' which Susan Barrowclough detects in recent feminist discourses on pornography ('all men react the same way, and all identify with the male point of view') needs to be watched out for in discussions of the reading as well as the viewing of pornography.[85] The same is true of her call for a discrimination of pornographies: 'various pornographies operate differently, cater to different audiences and elicit different sexual responses'. If so, the connection between pornography and rape may not be so unwaveringly deterministic as abolitionists believe. Traditionally, pornographic writing is better known as a stimulus to masturbatory reverie than as a combat manual for male rapists: 'it can be read only with one hand', quipped the Maréchale de Luxembourg.[86] Certainly, the pornographies which circulate among us include some directed specifically at women – not just the pornography of emotions on which Mills and Boon romances capitalise so successfully, nor even religious pornography like Colleen McCullough's *The thorn birds* (1977), which offers Roman Catholic women the vicarious thrills of sexual relations with a priest – but precisely the kind of pornography which in some feminist criticism is naively assumed to be for men only. But as Lesley Stern observes, 'it may well turn out that female fantasy is not singular and certainly contradictory, that the intertwinings of sex and death and violence are not uniquely male properties'.[87] A feminist intervention in pornography might therefore be difficult to engineer if it were to involve tampering not just with the circulation of unsavoury products but with modes of fantasising which are not the prerogative of one sex only.

In order to stabilise the pornographic as a suitable target of feminist attack it is necessary to have a uniform conception of it as a mode of representation in which women are degraded for the pleasure of men. And it would appear to be equally necessary to have a uniform conception of the recipient of pornographic materials as always a male who will be driven invariably (having, as the Victorians used to say, a 'beast' within him) to act out on real women the obscene and sadistic fantasies implanted in him by someone else's diseased imagination. As soon as you start to conceive of pornographies as a plurality, or to put in question the unity of the subject (reader or viewer, male or female) at whom those pornographies are directed, pornography will inevitably elude feminist critiques and become just another of those things which liberal humanists worry about if asked to draw the distinction between liberty and licence in the modes by which men and women are represented to one another.

The more polemical a feminist's motives are in investigating evidence of misogyny, the more likely it is that she will clash with non-feminists over the interpretation of a disputed text, especially if it happens to be the work of a canonical author. The disagreement between Sandra M. Gilbert and Joan Malory Webber over whether or not *Paradise lost* is a misogynistic and patriarchal poem epitomises the problems which arise when a committed feminist critic and an equally committed non-feminist scholar strive for possession of what is considered to be a classic of the English language.[88] To Webber, being a woman is secondary to being a scholar when it comes to talking about Renaissance texts: like Helen Gardner, she sees it as the business of historical scholarship to preserve Milton's text from the perversions of fashion, and by historicising it she is able to claim that Gilbert does not know enough or read carefully enough to be a reliable commentator on *Paradise lost*. But to Gilbert, who speaks for 'sensitive female readers', there is no such thing as a historically correct reading which is valid for all time. To read *Paradise lost* in the 1970s is a vastly different enterprise from reading it in the 1670s, and there is no point in disguising the fact that what women find so 'bruisingly real' about the poem is its representation of 'the historical dispossession and degradation of the female principle'. Its treatment of women is such as to make it vulnerable to the feminist criticism it deserves, no matter how improperly anachronistic a procedure that might appear in the eyes of Milton scholars. As a feminist reading of the poem, Gilbert's is revisionist, and reproduces *Paradise lost* as a work engaged in an unsatisfactory manner with one of the most sensitive issues of our own time; to Webber, Gilbert's reading is simply a misreading.

The wider context of this difference of opinion is the debate about what is entailed in doing a reading of something, and what degree of latitude is permissible in an activity which can never aspire to exactitude. Feminist criticism has benefited from the widespread sympathy given to the view that 'meaning' is not inherent in texts but is something manufactured for them by readers in the process of reading, and that what determines the relative correctness of an interpretation is consensus among a community of readers. Harold

Bloom's theory of 'creative misprision' − which is that young writers make room for themselves by wilfully misreading the writings of their predecessors, evading in that way disabling feelings of inferiority in the presence of past masters − gets applied to critics as well as to writers, particularly by those who think of criticism as a creative act.[89] The scholarly quest for correct readings is displaced by an interest in 'good misreadings' ('By a good misreading', Paul de Man explains, 'I mean a text that produces another text which can itself be shown to be an interesting misreading, a text which engenders additional texts').[90] Such an attitude suits marxists who think that a correct reading would be undesirable even if obtainable because it would bind a text repressively to one particular moment in its history. And it certainly suits feminist critics whose business is not to seek (as Webber does) the meaning of a text in the conditions in which it emerged originally, but to confer on it the kind of reading which enables (say) *Paradise lost* to have a feminist 'moment' in a post-Miltonic career conceived of as being the history of such moments.

Misreading (in de Man's sense) frequently operates by turning a work as it were inside out, in the way that D. H. Lawrence did when he rewrote the Revelation of St John in *Apocalypse* (London, 1931), transforming the biblical serpent from a symbol of death into a symbol of life, thus 'restoring' to the text a meaning allegedly removed from it by St John in his Christian interpretation of a pagan motif: *Apocalypse* is consequently Lawrence's revisionist reading of St John's revisionist reading of pagan symbolism. This is a procedure familiar in Robert Graves' studies of classical mythology, where the received version of a myth is seen as a 'mythotropic' reversal of the meaning encoded in some lost earlier version; and *The white goddess* (1948) is based on the theory that what we encounter in Celtic myth are traces of a matriarchal language which has been tampered with in the interests of a patriarchal society.[91]

In Graves' terms, Lawrence's rewriting of the Book of Revelation might be called 'semiotropic', since what are presented as negative signs in St John's text are 'turned' into positive signs in Lawrence's misreading of it. A well-known feminist instance of this sort of thing is Kate Millett's semiotropic reading of Charlotte Brontë's novel *Villette* (1853), which sees the heroine, Lucy Snowe, not as sadly deprived of marriage to Paul Emanuel at the end, but triumphantly saved from matrimony and given independence.[92] This reading is open to the same kind of objection which Webber directs (on the

'evidence' of the text) at Gilbert's reading of *Paradise lost*: Patricia M.
Spacks, for instance, thinks that the ending of *Villette* indicates that
Lucy will eventually marry Paul, and that 'the book Charlotte Brontë
wrote is even more interesting than the one Kate Millett invents'.[93] A
feminist riposte to this might be that relatively few people felt inclined
to read *Villette* until Millett 'misread' it in a way that made it appear
important: so what is to be gained by a 'correct' reading which makes
Villette seem just as conventional as any number of other novels written
in that period? 'No one who has read *Sexual politics*', Elaine Showalter
declares, 'can ever read *Villette* sentimentally again.'[94]

What could never be claimed for Millett's reading, however, even
if it were less tendentious than it is, is that it stabilises the meaning of
Villette, no matter how satisfying some feminists may find it. The
theory that every reading is a rewriting is consequently a mixed blessing
to feminists, who must face up to the fact that currently fashionable
feminist readings of this or that text will end up on the junk-heap of
history when future readers either ignore such texts or construct them
in such a way as to produce for them a new 'moment' in which they will
appear supremely relevant to what people at that time consider to be
supremely important. It cannot be assumed, in other words, that
feminist readings which at present liberate women's texts from
patriarchal bondage will themselves survive in perpetuity. Like
moralised versions of the myths in Ovid's *Metamorphoses* (or any other
remains from a defunct activity), they will arouse curiosity and wonder
– if they are noticed at all – among people who have other interests
in mind and other ways of spending their time.

4

Gynocritics

Most of the activities described in the previous chapter are the work of vigilantes who believe that before women can be liberated it is necessary to dismantle those parts of the androcentric culture which keep them in subjection. And seeing that language and literature are part of that culture, a feminist critic can contribute towards the de-centring of androcentrism by designating gender the principal criterion for assessing those dominant but usually unacknowledged conventions which determine how women speak and write.

Implicit in all such enterprises is a conviction that the work of demolition will be followed by a programme of rebuilding, whether it is the integrationist dream of a society from which gender stereotyping has been removed, or the separatist dream of a community of women as gynocentric as the present regime is androcentric, and perhaps with similar shortcomings. To think beyond the deconstruction of androcentrism therefore presents problems, for it is much easier to achieve consensus on what women are being liberated from — exploitation by men — than on what they are being liberated to, and Diana Trilling is not alone in her misgivings about recent novels of female self-realisation whose heroines find themselves 'liberated to a new tyranny' in their pursuit of sexual fulfilment.[1] Nevertheless, it is commonly agreed that the negative task of exposing androcentric biases against women in general and women writers in particular ought to be complemented by the more positive task of defining the specificity of women's writing. Indeed, it is said that the critique of androcentrism is itself a somewhat reactionary activity, because it keeps women dependent on male modes of writing and thinking about writing; for in order to dissent from androcentric premises you have to engage in dialectic with them, and to that extent you are compromised by permitting the grounds of the debate to be determined by those premises: time spent refuting men might be used more profitably promoting women. But in order to escape what Showalter calls 'the feminist obsession with correcting, modifying, supplementing, revising, humanizing, or even attacking male critical theory', you have to believe that women are capable of disinfecting their activities completely of all masculine reference, and that Simone de Beauvoir was unjustifiably pessimistic in thinking that whenever women 'band together in order to establish a counter-universe . . . they always set it up within the frame of the masculine universe'.[2]

Saying what something is not is easier than saying what it is, especially if you are dealing with a new field for which a descriptive vocabulary is still being devised. Attempting to describe the indescribable, Betty Friedan decided to make do with 'the problem that has no name', because *anomie* – 'that bored, diffuse feeling of purposelessness, non-existence, non-involvement with the world' – was not quite the right word for what middle-class American women were experiencing in the late 1950s.[3] Some believe that not having names for things scarcely matters, because if you are suffering from a problem you don't have to name it in order to suffer from it, or to recognise symptoms of it in fellow sufferers: 'naming' is thus construed as a masculine activity, a manifestation of that passion for organisational tidiness which, in seeking to 'master' reality by enclosing it in categories, ends up ignoring things which don't fit, such as problems without names. But others incline to the view that definitions and terminologies are not necessarily oppressive, and that if the terms you need in order to mobilise your discourse don't exist then you should feel free to invent them. In the case of literary studies, for instance, the negative task of deconstructing androcentrism can be called quite plausibly 'the feminist critique'; but the term is much less appropriate if applied to the correspondingly positive task of describing and analysing writing by women. Not until Showalter Englished *la gynocritique* as 'gynocritics' in 1979 was there a suitable word available to describe this positive side of the feminist critical enterprise, namely the study of 'woman as the producer of textual meaning'.[4] What this amounts to, as Showalter's 1981 definition makes clear, is a concern with 'women *as writers* . . . the history, styles, themes, genres, and structures of writing by women; the psychodynamics of female creativity; the trajectory of the individual or collective female career; and the evolution and laws of a female literary tradition'.[5]

That is an immense project which involves coordinating work done already in case-studies of individual writers or topics; doing again work which hasn't been done properly, usually because the investigators were themselves insufficiently alert to androcentric biases in their modes of enquiry; and doing work which has never been done before. The feminist critique of androcentric practices is a relatively circumscribed world in comparison with the expanding universe of gynocritics. This is mainly because androcentrism is a definable phenomenon whose manifestations are by no means infinite, no matter how devious they are in practice or multifarious in form. The feminist critique is a unified field because all its activities home in on the same despised centre. But 'women's writing' is a term which conceals various ideological rifts, one of which is revealed by Rosalind Coward's question: 'Are women's novels feminist novels?'[6] As such, women's writing is a dispersed field which cannot constitute the organising centre of gynocritics in quite the same uncomplicated way that androcentrism determines what constitutes the feminist critique. It is the recognition of this fact which inhibits anybody trying to map the new field — rather than the daunting amount of gynocritical materials to be surveyed, or the paranoid objection that the only reason anyone could have for wanting to define the gynocritical enterprise would be to circumscribe its limits in order to close it down.

ii

Whereas a feminist critique of language aims at revealing androcentric bias in linguistic practices, gynocritical enquiries focus on the specificity of 'woman's language'. This is the term used by Robin Lakoff in a pioneering study called 'Language and woman's place' (1973), the ironical title of which glances at Elizabeth Janeway's *Man's world, woman's place* (New York, 1971) and declares its alliance with the feminist critique, particularly in the support it gives to the view that 'the marginality and powerlessness of women is reflected in . . . the ways women are expected to speak'.[7] But the gynocritical contribution of Lakoff's essay is its attempt to specify certain lexical, syntactical and intonational features as characteristic of 'woman's language', and which have come to be known subsequently as 'WL features'. As a term, 'woman's language' is vulnerable of course to objections already mentioned to the setting up of 'woman' as an unchanging essence located outside of discourse, and in that respect 'women's language' would be a less contentious label for a phenomenon which in any case is disputed on sociolinguistic rather than semiotic grounds. But as the alternative descriptive terms are

either disparaging ('Sispeak') or whimsical ('sapphistry'), we may as
well stick with WL, as the initials neatly evade the woman/women
dispute.[8]

Among those who believe that language is irredeemably
androcentric, WL is conceived of sometimes as a non-verbal
communication system in which intimacies of touch replace the
duplicity of words. 'At some sisterhood get-togethers', Angela Carter
reports, 'the attempt at verbal intercourse is abandoned altogether in
favor of "touching rituals," tactile exchanges that bring those who
engage in them closer together than words can.'[9] Such highly
articulate accounts of inarticulacy point to the disingenuousness of
attempting to avoid the perfidy of language by pretending that bodily
contact is a pristine and unmediated expression of authentic feeling,
as if touch were incapable of being used (as words undoubtably are) for
insincere or exploitative purposes. Beyond communication by touch
alone lies that non-tactile form of communication by so-called body
language, misunderstandings of which can have such alarming
consequences, as witnessed in court testimonies concerning rape cases.
And at the outer limits of intra-feminine communication systems is a
zone of silent communion – not the silence imposed forcibly on
women by patriarchal practices which deny them a speaking position
in the dominant discourse, but 'the new sounds of silence', as Mary
Daly calls them, 'intersubjective silence, the vibrations of which are too
high for the patriarchal hearing mechanism . . . ultrasonic'.[10] This is
imagined to be something which women have a tacit knowledge of, and
which men not only cannot tune into, but are not even aware of. As a
site for the specificity of WL, however, what Daly is talking about is
not much use, for critical discourse is much better attuned to the noises
of articulation than to the sounds of silence.

Those who attempt to theorise the specificity of WL have very few
options when it comes to pin-pointing its origins. It must somehow
emerge after silence but before a girl has internalised the oppressor's
language in learning to speak; this restricts its provenance to the early
stages of infantile development. And in so far as WL can have only a
mental or a physical origin, the choice is between psychological theories
which locate it in the unconscious, and somatic theories which derive
it from the female body, usually from its genital characteristics.

In the simplest kind of psychoanalytic theory, the conscious use of
language is designated male and the unconscious female. This results
from a feminist appropriation of Freud's distinction between the

language of the unconscious, which uses images and puns as freely as poetry in creating those 'irrational' and ambiguous scenarios we call dreams, and that conscious, 'rational' and (we try to ensure) disambiguated language in which our daily affairs are conducted. In non-feminist discourse, Freud's account of the dream-work is read as one of the great defences of poetry, because it establishes the 'poetic' uses of language as endemic to the human mind and anterior to those 'logical' developments which have made European civilisation possible. But other constructions of it are clearly permissible, including one which would equate a repressed unconscious with a repressed femininity, and identify man the oppressor as the agent of repression. If so, then the dark continent of the unconscious is the place in which to search for an authentically feminine specificity. 'The writing of women', according to Marguérite Duras, 'is really translated from the unknown.'[11] She has in mind her own experience of those involuntary moments when the book she was busy with suddenly started, as it were, to write itself: 'I know that when I write . . . I let something take over inside me that probably flows from femininity.' At such moments, 'everything shuts off — the analytic way of thinking, thinking inculcated by college, studies, reading, experience. . . . It's as if I were returning to a wild country.' A Freudian explanation of such moments would be that a withdrawal of ego control permitted the release of unconscious materials which Duras then experienced as a surprising encounter with something other than her familiar self. What is questionable in her account, accordingly, is not the nature of the experience she records (for many writers, men as well as women, have left similar testimonies), but the assumption that what she had access to when invaded by her unconscious was an essential femininity inaccessible to the analytic and cognitive techniques she acquired in the course of being educated in a man's world. To validate Duras' interpretation of her involuntary experiences as a writer, it is therefore necessary to show that the development of the unconscious in women is so very different from the parallel process in men as to constitute something specifically female, one of the manifestations of which is identifiable as WL.

The most ambitious attempt to re-think for feminist purposes the psychoanalytic theory of language-acquisition is by Julia Kristeva in *La Révolution du langage poétique* (Paris, 1974). Her starting-point is Lacan's distinction between the Imaginary and the Symbolic. In the Imaginary, it will be recalled (see p. 63), the child experiences unity with its mother, and the price to be paid for the acquisition of language in the Symbolic (whose signifier is the phallus) is exile from the Imaginary. By treating Lacan's distinction between the Imaginary and the Symbolic as a difference between the maternal and the paternal, Kristeva is able to claim that the Lacanian model has a masculine bias to it, since it conceives of language as a unitary phenomenon confined to a Symbolic order whose characteristics are undeniably masculine. A possible feminist project, therefore, would be to demonstrate that that language which each of us acquires irrespective of our sex on entering the paternal Symbolic — and which we are encouraged to believe is the only language worth having, grown-ups' language — is in fact masculine language, which is why so many women experience it as alien or alienating. And furthermore, that that other language, ridiculed as baby-talk which we are expected to grow out of when we enter the Symbolic and grow up, is the non-dualistic and native language of the maternal Imaginary, a rhythmic babble which bonds mother with child and which might well be considered the matrix of a suppressed women's language.

But this is not the project Kristeva has in mind. In the course of revising Lacan, she redefines the Imaginary somewhat confusingly as *le sémiotique* (it is worth retaining the French term here, I think, as otherwise it is difficult to preserve in English Kristeva's distinction between *le sémiotique* and *la sémiotique*, 'semiotics'). *Le sémiotique* is an alternative mode of signification to the Symbolic. Its constitutive articulations are bundled together in what Kristeva, borrowing a term from Plato's *Timaeus*, calls the *chora* — 'a pre-verbal, pre-Oedipal locus' (in the words of Alice A. Jardine's helpful gloss) 'where the world is perceived by the child as rhythmic, intonational, melodic'.[12] This pre-verbal *chora* is 'anterior to [Symbolic] signification, denotation, syntax, the word, even the syllable': it is 'the primary organization of instinctual drives by rhythm [and] intonation', and 'functions in discourse as a supplementary register to that of the sign and meaning'.

Now if femininity is a construct effected in language, and language exists (according to Lacan's system) only in the paternal Symbolic, women end up losers no matter what subject position they adopt, for they can only be either pseudo-males or marginalised females. The advantage for women in Kristeva's system is that it places *le sémiotique* and the Symbolic not in an order of supercession (such that the first has to be abandoned before the second can be attained) but in an order of interaction. Interplay between *le sémiotique* and the Symbolic constitutes the subject in language, not as a fixity but as a subject-in-process (*sujet en procès*), which means that the *chora* can never be eliminated, no matter how much it is repressed. But the disadvantage for women in Kristeva's system is that the process she describes is not female-specific, because people who are biologically male are capable of taking up a 'feminine' subject-position in the Symbolic. Her evidence comes from 'avant-garde' writing produced by men like Joyce or Mallarmé, who jettison the formal structures of language codified in the Symbolic in order to explore what it excludes, namely those 'irrational' but evocative properties of sound and rhythm which stir memories of an older and largely forgotten order of signification whose original locus is the *chora*.

From Kristeva's position, therefore, it would be somewhat naive to conceive of the relationship between men and women as oppositional, for if women can be 'masculine' and men 'feminine' in negotiating the transaction between *le sémiotique* and the Symbolic, there is no point in isolating 'women' as a special category on biological grounds and inventing something called feminism to protect their interests. Kristeva's analysis of the construction of the subject in language, in other words, is too corrosive for comfort, for in deconstructing phallocratic theories of language acquisition she deconstructs feminism as well. This is why her work is approached warily by those who feel that women still need looking after in a patriarchy: the Marxist–Feminist Literature Collective, for instance, has misgivings about an argument such as Kristeva's which 'idealises and romanticises the discursive ruptures of the avant-garde' and 'risks privileging and feminising the irrational'.[13] One way of saving the Kristevan system, therefore, for a feminism conceived of as an oppositional practice in a phallocracy would be to take *le sémiotique* as constituting an alternative to the Symbolic, and to theorise WL in terms of the *chora*.

Somatic theories of the origin of language and writing treat the female body sometimes as the autonomous generator of WL and sometimes as a medium through which the unconscious finds expression. When Hélène Cixous says that 'writing is of the body', and that 'a woman does not write like a man, because she speaks with the body',[14] it would appear that she is taking sexual dimorphism − the structural difference between male and female genitals − as the source of that gendering of language and style which feminist modes of criticism try to define. But the point of persuading a woman to write with her body, it turns out, is to help her articulate her psychological femininity, so that 'the immense resources of [her] unconscious will spring forth' and 'the inexhaustible feminine imaginary will unfold'.[15] The only part of the body which seems to be involved regularly in such exercises, however, are the female genitals, which are much disparaged in a Freudian psychology that regards women as castrated men suffering from penis-envy. To display a sequence of vulvas for non-pornographic purposes — as Anne Severson did in her 'cunt movie', *Near the big chakra* (1972) — is therefore a revolutionary act in a patriarchal culture; for as Cathy Schwichtenberg observes, 'vulva after vulva teases at any ultimate, satiated signification'.[16] Similarly, to write from the vulva is to acknowledge as positive an organ classified as negative in a dominantly androcentric psychology which privileges the penis rather than the vulva as the marker of sexual dimorphism.[17] In other words, a woman should write with what she has got, instead of feeling (after listening to all those men who claim to have written with their penises) that she lacks the necessary wherewithal.

An explicit attempt to link feminine discourse with the structure of the female genitals occurs in the writings of Luce Irigaray, who treats morphological differences between the sexual organs as the source of such 'masculine' characteristics as the preoccupation with correct meanings and a unified subject, and 'feminine' characteristics like process, plurality and diversity. She argues that because 'all Western discourse presents a certain isomorphism with the masculine sex', an alternative discourse in which women have the dominant voice must emanate from the vulva rather than the penis.[18] From a phallocentric point of view, the vulva is important only as the entrance to the vagina, which is thought of as 'imperfect' until penetrated by a penis.[19] But in Irigaray's account, which is '*con*centric' in Gallop's sense ('cunt-centric'), the vulva is already complete in itself on account of the labia, those 'two lips which embrace each other continuously', and which ensure that every woman is 'in touch with herself by herself and in herself': what interferes with this auto-erotic pleasure is 'the brutal separation of these two lips by a penis/violator'.[20] In somatic terms, the definition of feminine sexuality is therefore 'that sex which is not one': the labia make it 'always twofold at least' and therefore '*plural* as well'. The consequence of this (in Carolyn Burke's summary) is that 'women's language will be plural, autoerotic, diffuse, and undefinable within the familiar rules of (masculine) logic'.[21]

A good deal depends here on the accuracy of Irigaray's characterisation of the penis as 'one' in comparison with the 'not one' of the vulva. Certainly, her theory seems to require the penis to be always inflexibly erect and quite without metamorphic variation, and also to be circumcised, as the presence of a foreskin endows it with most of the properties she attributes to the labia. Perhaps the terms of Irigaray's argument should not be treated in so crudely literal a fashion, but it is not only men who think she operates with too narrow a conception of female sexuality. 'What is the meaning of "two lips" to heterosexual women who want men to recognize their clitoral pleasure', asks Ann Rosalind Jones, 'or to African or Middle Eastern women who, as a result of pharaonic clitoridectomies, have neither lips nor clitoris through which to *jouir*?'[22] But there are other problems here, as there are with any version of the argument that women communicate better with their bodies than with their heads. For one thing, it plays into the hands of antifeminists who are only too ready to disparage women on biologistic grounds; for another, as the editorial collective of *Questions féministes* points out, 'there is no such thing as a direct relation to the body', which means that whatever the body 'says' is mediated inevitably through language.[23] It is true that the female 'speaking body' is commonly encountered in the literary tradition, but usually in representations which most feminists would regard as sexist, and which therefore cast doubts on the feasibility of writing the body feminine without evoking undesirable associations. English readers of Cixous and Irigaray are likely to be reminded of the way women's bodies are used by male Romantic writers when troping poetic discourse as an alternative to logical discourse, as in the case of W. B. Yeats' poem 'Michael Robartes and the dancer' (1921), in which the idea that women silently 'speak' with their bodies a wisdom unattainable by men is used as an argument for not educating them in masculine ways of thinking. Moreover, the masculine tradition that women speak with their sexual organs is not only reactionary but disparagingly comic, and I imagine that readers of Cixous would prefer not to be reminded of Diderot's *Les Bijoux indiscrets* (1748), in which the vulvas of various women are induced to confess their experiences by means of a magic ring which confers on them the powers of speech.[24] It is therefore a dubious move in the face of all this to urge women to speak their own bodies '*con*centrically'.

Anglophone investigators, by contrast, take a much more empirical approach to WL, and are correspondingly more interested in what might be considered evidence of its existence than in framing psychosomatic theories of its origin. The point of departure for recent debates on this topic is Lakoff's 1973 essay on 'Language and woman's place', which attempts to list some of the criterial features of WL phonologically, grammatically and semantically. In the matter of lexical choice, for instance, she claims that only women ever use words like 'sweet' and 'divine' to convey non-ironical approbation. 'Talking like a lady' means blunting the edge of declarative statements by encasing them in modifiers ('I think that perhaps what we want is to be strong women'); it also involves uttering declarative statements with an interrogative intonation, especially in sentences ending in so-called tag questions ('That's the correct term for them, isn't it?'), and eschewing the 'rough' speech of men by speaking hypercorrectly ('my girlfriend and I'). As a contribution to the feminist critique, Lakoff's essay provides evidence of the link between deferential speech-habits and the insecurity of women in a man's world, and her purpose is to clarify the nature of the double-bind in which WL places a woman: 'If she refuses to talk like a lady, she is ridiculed and subjected to criticism as unfeminine; if she does learn, she is ridiculed as unable to think clearly, unable to take part in a serious discussion: in some sense, as less than fully human.'[25] But gynocritically, Lakoff wants linguists to admit that a unitary conception of the grammatical is inadequate. For if 'a sentence that is "acceptable" when uttered by a woman is "unacceptable" when uttered by a man', there must be 'hierarchies of grammaticality', one of the constraints on which is 'the social context in which the utterance is expressed, and the assumptions about the world made by all the participants in the discourse'.[26]

Before feminists took an interest in it, WL was conceived of by Europeans as either mythic or exotic. On the one hand it was a matriarchal phenomenon which had vanished in prehistoric times with the institution of patriarchy, but which had left its traces in various myths and ritual practices; and on the other hand it was believed to be a characteristic of distant but 'primitive' peoples like the Caribs, which European travellers had first reported in 1664.[27] It is ironical that the most intricate reconstruction of an extinct WL should have been undertaken by Robert Graves, a male chauvinist in the eyes of many feminists on account of his view that women can never be true poets because their business is to be muses and inspire male poets. Nevertheless, it is Graves' contention in *The white goddess* (London, 1948) that poetic language derives from a magical language in honour of the moon goddess, traces of which are to be found in Old Welsh and

Old Irish myths and poems. None of this is taken seriously by linguists, of course, who regard *The white goddess* as having the same sort of function with respect to Graves' poetry as *A vision* does to the poetry of W. B. Yeats, that is, as a privately manufactured mythology out of which poems can be made. Exotic WL, on the other hand, attracted the attention of various turn-of-the-century scholars whose speculations about it have not been taken seriously since Otto Jespersen pointed out in 1922 that the apportioning of selected lexical items to one sex but not the other as a result of verbal taboos does not warrant thinking of the consequences as two separate languages, especially as only about ten per cent of the vocabulary is affected by such practices.[28]

Since the 1960s, however, we have witnessed a renewed interest in mythic WL – not as something which has to be pieced together from a lost arcadian past, but as something imaginable in utopias of the future, like those depicted in novels such as Marge Piercy's *Woman on the edge of time* (New York, 1976) and Sally Miller Gearhart's *The wanderground* (Watertown, 1979), or set out in dictionary fashion by Monique Wittig and Sande Zeig in *Lesbian peoples* (New York, 1979).[29] The kind of WL in which Lakoff is interested, by contrast, already exists in the here and now, and can be described by a linguistics modified along feminist lines. Not surprisingly, her critics are as reluctant as Jespersen would have been to concede that the differences she points to in the ways men and women speak constitute evidence for the existence of separate languages. But if WL is not a language, then what is it? Seeing that we call regional versions of standard English 'dialects' and class versions 'sociolects', should we conceive of English as having what Wayne Dickerson calls 'genderlects'?[30] This would be permissible if the criterial features of WL never turned up in men's language; but of course they do, and even Kramarae has to concede that 'probably few, if any, of the language usages discussed . . . are particular to either females or males'.[31] WL features are therefore not so much 'sex-exclusive' as 'sex-preferential', to use Ann Bodine's distinction.[32] The most which can be claimed of any of them is that it is more common in the speech of women than of men, but nevertheless not so common as to be characteristic of the speech of all women. From a linguistic point of view, differences between WL and men's language turn out to be less noticeable than those between 'standard' English and certain types of black English. In any case, it might be questioned what political use there is in arguing that 'underneath' or 'inside' man-made language is a female-specific language which ought to be granted the

kind of attention currently given to any protected species. For if
the characteristics of WL signify not so much 'femaleness' as
'powerlessness', women have more to gain politically from increasing
their authority in the discourses of power than in widening the gap
between the oppressor's language and their own by proposing WL as
some sort of alternative to it.

What emerges from responses to Lakoff's claims is that the
phenomenon she tried to describe is slightly different from what she
thought it was, and that more factors are involved than she took
account of.[33] Experiments have made it clear that what one says is
affected by the sex of the person addressed, and that intragender
discourse, woman to woman, does not display the same characteristics
as intergender discourse, woman to man. The conditions in which
verbal exchanges occur also influence the forms they take to such an
extent that gender cannot be isolated from the bundle of features which
constitute the context of any speech act. The gendering of the subject
in discourse may have no connection whatsoever with the sex of the
person who occupies that subject-position, which is why George Eliot
can be said to write like a man, and E. M. Forster like a woman. But
as working women who have to deal with men testify, if you happen
to look like a woman you may very well be heard as one, even if you
go out of your way to avoid prejudice by resolutely not talking 'like a
woman'.

What Lakoff got on to, therefore, was not a genderlect but rather
what Sally McConnell-Ginet calls 'communicative strategies mediated
by gender/sex systems'.[34] These 'interact with language not because
they are somehow part of a grammar, but because they play a critical
role in shaping beliefs and influencing the actions involved in
using that grammar for linguistic communication'. This is as
good a way as any of sustaining gynocritical interest in the
WL phenomenon, and avoiding the double-bind Lakoff got herself
into, and which Eleanor Kuykendall puts like this: 'either what
she calls women's language cannot be described as specifically
female, or what speakers know cannot be described as knowledge
of the language'.[35]

To shift attention from how women speak to how they write raises
the literary critical question of whether there is such a thing as a
feminine style of writing, the nuclear model of which is what Virginia
Woolf called 'a woman's sentence'.[36]

iii

The grouping together of women writers for the purposes of literary study rests on the questionable principle that 'being a woman' is somehow different from being (say) a Quaker or a parvenu or one of any number of other types of people whose classification is determined by the application of some categorial distinction such as class or religious denomination. The latter are thought of as cultural classifications, whereas being a woman is not: difference of sex is believed to be a matter of Nature, not of Culture, and must 'surely' make for differences in style, since what you write is what you are (*le style c'est la femme même*), and women are women, not non-men. 'It is not that everything women do as poets is different from what men do', Suzanne Juhasz argues, 'or that women use words in ways that men don't, or can't, but that many of their ways are different, and that their ways are for the purpose of expressing in art their real selves, not the selves that have been created for them.'[37] This commonsense assertion of what any reasonable person would take to be obvious — 'that there *is* something unique about women's writing'[38] — is of course not the end of the matter but merely an incentive to gynocritical enquiries into whether or not it is true, and if so, in what ways women's writing may be said to differ from men's.

Some women writers think the question pointless because the commonsense view is simply wrong. 'The serious artistic voice is one of individual style, and it is sexless', according to Joyce Carol Oates.[39] Others find the enquiry theoretically naive, on the grounds that once you have questioned the idea of a unified subjectivity (as you must if you take Lacanian psychoanalysis seriously) you cannot then behave as if sexual identity remained miraculously intact. 'I do not find it easy to define a masculine or feminine specificity', Kristeva writes, 'when I think of the great aesthetic experiences of the decentering of identity.'[40]

Kristeva's comment comes uncharacteristically close here to statements by people who relate writing to something called 'the creative imagination', the sex of which is said to be neither masculine nor feminine but androgynous. Coleridge's remark (dated 1 September 1832) that 'a great mind must be androgynous' caught the attention of Virginia Woolf, who glossed it as meaning that 'perhaps a mind that is purely masculine cannot create, any more than a mind that is purely feminine'.[41] As Woolf presents it, creative androgyny looks very much like one of those myths of complementarity which feminists are rightly suspicious of: male writers, according to Woolf, depend on 'the woman part of the brain', just as 'a woman also must have intercourse with the man in her'. Confirmation of this claim is said to come, as might be expected, from Shakespeare, who is described as 'the type of the androgynous, of the man–womanly mind'. Woolf's critics, noting the unequivocal presence of androgynous themes in *Orlando* (1928) and more subtle workings of them in some of the other novels, have interpreted her own writings together with those of other members of the Bloomsbury group as examples of the 'androgynous vision'.[42]

To people who look beyond intersexual strife, androgyny figures as an ideal alternative to the social iniquities of sex-role stereotyping, which is why it turns up in utopian fictions such as Ursula Le Guin's *The left hand of darkness* (1969) and *The dispossessed* (1974). But others fear that androgyny is merely 'the sexist myth in disguise', because what it turns out to involve in practice is not some pure equilibrium of the sexes on the far side of gender discrimination, but the annexation of the female by the male in order to make the male more versatile and therefore more powerful.[43] Even the name itself is suspect to Adrienne Rich, who believes that 'the very structure of the word replicates the sexual dichotomy and the priority of *andros* (male) over *gyne* (female)'.[44] Empirical investigations reveal that male writers who are admired for their androgynous sympathies cannot always survive the kind of scrutiny which Anne K. Mellor directs at Blake, whose 'theoretical commitment to androgyny in his prophetic books', she concludes, 'is . . . undermined by his habitual equation of the female with the subordinate or the perversely dominant'.[45] Consequently, androgyny is regarded currently as much more of a cul-de-sac in feminist studies than was the case a few years ago, and its marginalisation has simplified considerably the debate about whether or not men and women write differently from one another.

Unless the terms of that debate are framed very carefully, it appears to embody an irreconcilable contradiction. For on the one hand we encounter the 'cultural' argument that there are no essential or natural differences between men and women on which to base a gender-stylistics; but on the other hand we are told it is wrong to apply androcentric criteria when criticising women's writing because women are different from men and write differently. Furthermore, it would be inauthentic of a woman to try to write like a man merely to win the approval of male critics and avoid being on the receiving end of those patronising and disparaging comments which are the staple of what Mary Ellmann calls 'phallic criticism'.[46] One way out of this impasse is to argue that women write the way they do not because of what they are (the essentialist fallacy) but because of what they are constrained to be in a male-dominated society. The difficulty here is that femininity then has to compete with other influences on style, some of which may be more powerful. This is shown, for example, in Linda Nochlin's observation that although Dorothy Richardson 'consciously set out to create a female style and imagery', what she ends up giving us is merely 'a middle-class Englishwoman's experience and sensibility' — the articulation of class values, in other words, rather than of femininity.[47]

The search for distinctive features in writing by women is conducted with varying degrees of refinement. Much of it is impressionistic; and given the widespread belief that women are forcibly silenced in a patriarchy, it is perhaps not surprising that many readers should pick on 'voice' as the index of femininity. Reading Olive Schreiner, Showalter hears 'that voice, soft, heavy, continuous, [which] is a genuine accent of womanhood, one of the chorus of secret voices speaking out of our bones, dreadful and irritating but instantly recognizable'.[48] Voice tends to be linked with the intimacies of touch, and set up in contradistinction to a masculine preoccupation with looking and distancing. 'The female voice is first of all not objective or analytical', according to Anne Sexton. 'The "I" of the woman's poetic voice will be visible more often because the defenses which make the male more objective are not part of the female acculturation process.'[49]

Released from an enforced silence, the feminine voice is recognisable immediately by its fluency. Men have always known this, and mocked women's propensity for 'nattering on', not realising that intersexual conversations would be even more difficult than they are at present if women were not prepared to do what Pamela M. Fishman calls the 'interactional shitwork' which keeps them going.[50] To laud fluency as a feminine characteristic is therefore a brave attempt at transvaluing sexist clichés not only about women's speech but also about women's writing, which Virginia Woolf conceded was 'often chattering and garrulous — mere talk spilt over paper and left to dry in pools and blots'.[51] By a semiotropic rearrangement, such vices can be reconstructed as virtues. If women are derided for gossiping, Patricia Meyer Spacks will write in praise of gossip as a social catalyst; and if

Arnold Bennett characterises feminine style by 'its lack of restraint, its wordiness, and the utter absence of feeling for form' (he was thinking of George Eliot at the time), then Hélène Cixous will declare that 'a feminine textual body can be recognised by the fact that it is always without end, has no finish'.[52] Prolixity authenticates femininity. Leslie B. Tanner, prefacing an anthology of women's writings called, significantly, *Voices from women's liberation* (New York, 1971), confesses that she has done 'very little editing and cutting of material' because she wants 'to allow women's voices to be heard as they are without conforming to man-made rules of professionalism' (p. 14).

At an opposite extreme from impressionism is the type of analysis Mary P. Hiatt undertook with the aid of a computer, principally with the aim of testing the validity of the view commonly encountered in phallic criticism that men's writing is 'terse, rational, controlled, balanced, and strong', whereas women's is 'vapid, silly, hysterical, hyperemotional, [and] shrill'.[53] This involved selecting 100 contemporary books, fifty by men and fifty by women, and within each category twenty-five works of fiction and twenty-five of non-fiction. Four passages of 500 words were chosen to give a sample of 2000 words for each book and of 200,000 words for the whole project. Eight computer programmes were then designed to deal with such matters as 'sentence length; the use of parallel constructions; similes; certain adverbs, verbs and adjectives; rhetorical devices of repetition; and particular types of punctuation'. It is not clear what precautions were taken to guarantee the statistical significance of the results.[54] Nor is it clear how her objectively produced data is connected with the popular psychologising which sometimes accompanies it, as when she says that the comparatively high incidence of the word 'really' among women writers indicates that they are 'afflicted by doubts as to their credibility'.[55] Not much interest is taken in the question of whether the formal features identified in such an enquiry are constitutive of those effects − real or imaginary − which prompt the stereotypical labelling of writing as masculine or feminine. Exactly which formal features of style, for instance, could be said to produce effects which a phallic critic would label 'silly' or 'hysterical'? There is a strong likelihood that the sources of phallic criticism are not minutiae of style but extra-stylistic prejudices about women of the sort displayed by Theodore Roethke in a lengthy catalogue of the 'aesthetic and moral shortcomings' of women's poetry, which include 'the embroidering of trivial themes', 'carrying on excessively', and 'lamenting the lot of the woman', but none of the rhetorical or stylistic features which Hiatt is concerned with.[56] What she concludes, however, is what many women are pleased to hear, namely that there is indeed a feminine style as distinct from a masculine one, and that commonly held opinions about both are wrong, because women's writing is not only less verbose than men's but also more moderate in tone.

As a rhetorical performance masquerading as science, Hiatt's book is consequently more effective as a contribution to the feminist critique of androcentric prejudices than as a gynocritical enquiry into the way women write. And although this is in some ways disappointing, her book directs attention (because of the difficulties it encounters with its topic) to the possibility that stylistics is not the solution to the problem of 'feminine style', which is traditionally a locus of suppositions about the way women write or ought to write in order to be recognisable as women. If the problem we are dealing with is merely hearsay unencumbered with evidence — assumptions about women rather than responses to stylistic features — it may well be that we have been misled by the term 'feminine style' into believing that what is at issue are notions of 'style', and that what is needed therefore is a stylistics capable of identifying the distinctive features of women's writing. But if what we are dealing with are principally notions of 'the feminine' (displaced, in this case, on to 'style'), then there is something to be said for shifting the grounds of the enquiry from intrinsic to extrinsic considerations. Instead of asking what women's writing is, we should ask what it is thought to be, which means taking account of how it is received. There are two ways of doing this: one is by studying the history of the reception of books written by women, and the other is by conducting empirical investigations into what assumptions people make about a piece of writing if the sex of its author is withheld from them.

Of prime importance in this respect are books written by women but published pseudonymously and then reviewed by men, like *Wuthering Heights*, which Emily Brontë published in 1847 under the name of 'Ellis Bell', a name chosen (according to her sister Charlotte) on account of its sexual indeterminacy. 'The object of anonymity', wrote the author of *Adam Bede* (1859) — a woman who is known nowadays only by her pseudonym, George Eliot — 'was to get the book judged on its own merits, and not prejudiced as the work of a woman.'[57] But the point of choosing a male pseudonym as against publishing anonymously ('By a Lady', which is how Jane Austen's first published novel, *Sense and sensibility*, was presented in 1811) is to write from a position of power in a patriarchal society. Most reviewers of *Wuthering Heights*, having only the novel itself on which to base a judgement, assumed it to be the work of a man and valued it accordingly, thus validating Carol Ohmann's contention 'that there is a considerable correlation between what readers assume or know the sex of the writer to be and what they actually see, or neglect to see, in "his" or her work'.[58] The thing to do if you were a male reviewer was to scan the novel at hand for 'characteristics' which betrayed the sex of its author and, if the aggregate of them was on balance female, to review the book in those tones of more or less polite condescension — 'the mere twaddle of graciousness' — deemed appropriate when dealing with what George Eliot (writing anonymously this time) had called 'silly novels by lady novelists'.[59] Showalter has reconstructed the criteria used in such exercises, few of which could be considered even remotely stylistic.[60] If a text manifested power, breadth, distinctness, clarity, learning, knowledge of life, and so on, it was obviously the work of a man; you could pick a woman writer, on the other hand, by her refinement, tact, precision of observation, edifying manner and knowledge of domestic details. Significantly, many of the characteristics of women writers were negative ones: they lacked originality and education, for instance, and were unable to handle abstract thought; they were humourless, prejudiced, excessively emotional and (unpardonably) unable to create male characters convincingly.

Ohmann's analysis of Emily Brontë in the hands of male critics is assumed to be so typical that relatively little feminist work has been done in 'reception-studies'. Yet much remains to be investigated, and we should not assume too readily that the only reason a woman has for writing pseudonymously is to get a fair hearing in a man's world. 'By the end of the [nineteenth] century the pseudonym had become mere affectation', Vineta Colby reports. 'Mrs Pearl Craigie called herself John Oliver Hobbes because she published her first novel [*Some emotions and a moral*, 1891] in Unwin's Pseudonym Library and had to supply a pseudonym to qualify.'[61] It would be worth extending Ohmann's approach to take account of the reception of other women who wrote as men, such as Katherine Harris Bradley and her niece Edith Emma Cooper, who wrote several volumes of tragedies and poems under the name of 'Michael Field'; and also of men who wrote under women's names, like William Sharp, whose Celtic poems signed 'Fiona Macleod' persuaded W. B. Yeats to name the new movement in poetry Celtic rather than Irish. And if the case of the Brontës is so very typical of male hostility to women writers, it would be worth knowing why it is that in the latter half of the eighteenth century (according to Robert Halsbrand) 'novels were sometimes dishonestly attributed to women authors because a book by a woman was regarded as more salable than one by a man'.[62]

If diachronic studies of the reception of books by women are complemented by investigations into the way we read now, it immediately becomes obvious that we are no better than Victorian critics were at guessing the sex of authors from their writings, although we are probably on the look-out for different things. The method used in empirical investigations of our ability to sex a text is one made famous by I. A. Richards in *Practical criticism* (1929), which involves soliciting comments on passages of prose and verse from which titles, dates and names of authors have been removed. The original purpose of this exercise was to test people's ability to extract from the 'words on the page' everything they needed to know in order to understand and evaluate the passage, without being cued by extrinsic bits of information. And whenever the experiment is repeated, people always perform as badly as Richards' own students did – so badly, in fact, as to elicit the objection that the only thing proved by this experiment is the utter uselessness of its method, because nowhere outside an examination room is anybody ever obliged to treat a bit of decontextualised text as if it were somehow self-explanatory. Feminist versions of Richards' experiment are therefore doomed to repeat its ineptitudes. Jennifer Strauss discovered that only twenty-four of her students were able to identify correctly as the work of a man some unsigned poems by A. D. Hope; forty-six identified the author as female.[63] When Naomi Weisstein observed that only four out of twenty graduates, after six weeks' study of differences between men and women, could separate thematic apperception tests written by women from those written by men, she concluded in the students' favour that they were judging correctly by incorrect criteria.[64] If we did as badly as this in our everyday lives when trying to tell the difference between men and women we might well suspect there was something wrong with us. So either we have a long way to go before becoming as sensitive to textual as we are to bodily signals of sexuality, or textual signals of sexuality are rare to the point of being non-existent. Yet we are still as alarmingly ready as Victorian critics were to base value-judgements on fallacious assumptions about the sex of an author, as Philip Goldberg discovered when he found that women students tended to rate an essay highly if they believed that a man had written it, but not if it was attributed to a woman writer.[65]

The minimal unit for sexing a piece of writing is usually taken to be the sentence. This is because of the distinction Virginia Woolf makes between the 'man's sentence' (behind which 'one can see Johnson, Gibbon and the rest', and which is 'unsuited for a woman's use') and the 'woman's sentence', which Jane Austen knew about but George Eliot did not.[66] Because the man's sentence is designed to articulate certitudes and be the voice of authority, it is said to be much less flexible than the woman's sentence, which is 'capable of stretching to the extreme, of suspending the frailest particles, of enveloping the vaguest shapes',[67] and is, in short, not unlike Woolf's own sentences, or those encountered in the late novels of Henry James. Because of its subtlety, the woman's sentence needs to be protected against repressive punctuation: 'feminine prose', according to Dorothy Richardson, 'should properly be unpunctuated, moving from point to point without formal obstructions'.[68] A more aggressive expression of this attitude is to be found in Andrea Dworkin's attack on the publisher of her first book, *Woman hating* (1974), for having 'filled the pages with garbage: standard punctuation', but who was persuaded nevertheless to let her include an appendix denouncing 'the Immovable Punctuation Typography Structure', which 'aborts freedom, prohibits invention, and does us verifiable harm'.[69]

Richardson's most attentive critic, Gillian E. Hanscombe, thinks her author was searching for 'an open-ended mode' of writing sensitive enough 'to suggest the nature of experience itself, which is necessarily open-ended in the real world'.[70] By assuming that being open-ended is more or less the same as being female, Hanscombe manages to discuss Richardson's technical innovations in fiction (she was a pioneer, with James Joyce, of the stream-of-consciousness technique, although she abhorred the term) as if they were the expressive devices of an exclusively female consciousness. But a major problem with feminist theories of style which designate 'openness' or 'process' as specifically feminine features (by contrast with that preference for closure which is said to characterise masculine modes of writing) is that they can always be illustrated from texts by James Joyce, especially *Finnegans wake* (1939). There we encounter a type of language which resists closure by refusing to make the kind of exclusions which enable ordinary sentences to deal with one thing at a time. The openness of 'indergoading him on to the vierge violetian' can be closed into 'hindering and goading him on to the verge of violation', but only if we dismantle each neologism or portmanteau word and treat its component parts as options, only one of which we are allowed to choose.[71] Consequently, 'indigo' disappears from 'hinder-goading' just as 'violet' does from 'violetian'; and 'vierge' must be unravelled as either 'virgin' (French *vierge*) or 'verge'. The phonemic system which obliges us to make a paradigmatic choice between /et/ and /ate/ so as not to confuse 'violet' with 'violate' is replicated at other levels in those syntagmatic chains we call sentences, each of which normally excludes infinitely more than it includes. The language of *Finnegans wake* reverses this tendency, and is structured in such a way as to prevent us from hurrying along the syntagmatic line in order to pick up a fixed meaning at the end of each sentence. Instead, we are obliged to dally *en route* among those paradigmatic alternatives which the puns and nonce-words refuse to repress. It is hard to imagine anything more open-ended than that.

None of this is troublesome if you are willing to argue, as Cixous and Kristeva do, that some dominant forms of avant-garde writing are 'feminine' despite the fact that they have been produced by men. But it is no help whatsoever to the separatist argument that sentences express consciousness, and that the function of a woman's sentence, as Woolf said, is 'to describe a woman's mind', not a man's.[72] It is clear from the case of Samuel Richardson's *Clarissa*, however, that the word 'feminine' when applied to writing denotes an effect rather than an origin, and consequently throws more light on the assumptions of readers than on the sex of the author. Richardson did not have to be female in order to produce, stylistically, those gender-effects which made people think he writes 'like a woman'. What he did was to write in a way that contemporaries believed women write, and among those who were convinced by this manoeuvre were large numbers of admiring female readers.

Difficulties encountered in the quest for a female-specific style of writing lend support to the semiotic view that 'woman' is not something which pre-exists human discourses but on the contrary is a product of them: having no pre-discursive and specifically female 'essence', she has nothing to express in an essentially female way, and so there can be nothing essentially female for a style-researcher to locate. In addition, 'style' is a misleadingly unitary concept, given the diversity of stylistic practices: it would be impossible to reduce the diversity of styles in books written by men to a monolithic 'masculine' style capable of being contrasted with some equally monolithic 'feminine' style, which in turn would represent the full range of styles in books written by women. 'Are there any literary qualities present in all works by women and absent from all works by men?' asks Minda Rae Amiran, confident that the answer will be 'No.'[73] And the same conclusion is drawn by critics of other media. In connection with the visual arts, for instance, Lucy Lippard reports that 'there is no technique, form, or approach used exclusively by women'; and with respect to films, Stephen Heath concludes that 'it is impossible . . . to specify marks of cinematic enunciation that could *only* appear in films made by women'.[74]

Yet the supposition that sex and style are linked symbiotically is remarkable persistent, and results in feminist 'explanations' of stylistic phenomena which are notable for their boldness if nothing else. They avoid being queried, presumably, because they tell many feminists the sorts of things they like to hear; and they raise once more the question of why it is that feminist criticism is not more tolerant of equally plausible but non-feminist explanations of the phenomena it deals with. Consider, for example, Carolyn G. Heilbrun's response to a memorable sentence in Virginia Woolf's *To the lighthouse*, which reads: 'Mr Ramsay, stumbling along a passage one dark morning, stretched his arms out, but Mrs Ramsay having died rather suddenly the night before, his arms, though stretched out, remained empty.' On the lookout for sexism in syntax, Heilbrun notes that although it is Mrs Ramsay who does the dying, the subject of the sentence is nevertheless her husband, and that 'Mrs Ramsay exists only in a subordinate clause, the object of his needs.'[75] Woolf is read here through the spectacles of Simone de Beauvoir, who argues that women are caught up in a sort of social syntax in which they are never the Subject but always the Other. Heilbrun does not consider the possibility that Woolf may have decentred her own prose deliberately here for the rhetorical effect of imitative form, revealing unexpectedly in her sentence the unexpectedness of Mrs Ramsay's death. Woolf's casualness is as calculated as that displayed by E. M. Forster when handling the death of Leonard Bast in *Howards End* (1910). Some readers find Forsterian understatement excessively mannered, but nobody has ever supposed it to be a syntactical clue to the class-relationships explored in that novel. In each case there is an element of play with narrative expectations — a determination not to give the subject-matter its proper dues for fear of sounding melodramatic — rather than a politicising of syntactical structures. Heilbrun's comment tells us less about Woolf's narrative subtlety than about the kind of readers Heilbrun has in mind.

Every mode of criticism is at risk from those who practise it, and so it is important not to judge critical theory entirely by critical practice. Ineptitudes displayed in various feminist analyses of literary texts may well prompt misgivings about the people who write them, but don't constitute evidence that the central hypothesis of feminist literary criticism — that gender is a crucial determinant in the production, circulation and consumption of literary discourses — is wrong. What they make clear, however, is that this hypothesis can be supported only in terms of culturally derived notions of 'masculinity' and 'femininity' held in common by readers and writers. It cannot be supported in terms of stylistic features unique to the literary productions of one sex.

iv

'Gender' and 'genre' are frequently paired words in the feminist critique, and are encountered most often in connection with the complaint that women have at their disposal far fewer of the traditional literary genres than men have always had, and continue to have. Feminists claim that because most of the writing which has found its way into print is the work of men, what constitutes the bulk of western literature is androcentric, and therefore any attempt to sort it into 'kinds' or genres is bound to result in the slotting of male-centred works into male-defined categories. The business of a feminist critique is therefore to reveal masculine bias in the most familiar genres. Epic poems can be shown to articulate a masculine form of aggressive behaviour by celebrating the exploits of male warriors in ways repulsive to the women's peace movement; tragedy appears to be grounded in a patriarchal view of family structures; pastoral is a form of nostalgia peculiar to urban males; and so on. Such investigations overlap with gynocritics in showing what happens when a genre traditionally associated with men, such as the *Bildungsroman* (which traces the formative development of a male hero), gets taken over by women; or when a number of new works appear to have so many features in common as to make it feasible to think of them as constituting a new genre.

As a classification system for reducing the diversity of literature to manageable proportions in order to study it, genre is equivalent in the humanities to taxonomy in the natural sciences, and was in fact the first attempt ever made to systematise texts for literary study. It operated by the displacement of class-bias into literary forms, and resulted in a hierarchical model which made epic and tragedy 'naturally' superior to pastoral, because the first two genres, unlike the third, dealt exclusively with the goings-on of upper-class characters. Generic classification was consolidated as a result of being institutionalised for hundreds of years in a schooling system based on the belief that the best way of teaching boys to write well (girls seemed hardly worth the effort) was to make them study and imitate classical Latin authors. Each genre had its characteristic markers which were determined by criteria of appropriateness or 'decorum', because what was considered appropriate in one genre might be quite inappropriate in another. Generic markers functioned first as cueing devices to remind readers what kind of text they were dealing with, and secondly to facilitate judgement, since it was considered improper to judge something written in one genre by criteria drawn from another. Benefits were to be had from such a system, because it enabled writers to manipulate generic expectations for witty or surprising effects, as we see time and again in Shakespeare's works. But the strain of attempting to confine writing within the grids of a generic taxonomy is manifest not only in Shakespeare's mockery of 'tragical-comical-historical-pastoral' plays (*Hamlet*, II ii) but also in those genre-breaking activities which resulted in the development of 'mixed' genres such as tragicomedy, and which is so striking a feature of postmodern American fiction, with its indifference to generic distinctions between factual reporting and fictional invention, autobiographies and novels, and so on. Genre-breaking is a perpetual incitement to *homo taxonomicus* to invent new classification systems capable of reducing the Many if not to the One then at least to the Few. And when Paul Hernadi last surveyed them in 1972 he discovered sixty or so modern theories of genre, none of which had been constructed along gender lines.[76]

This may surprise people who expect to find the meaning of things in the etymologies of the words which describe them. 'Gender and genre come from the same root', notes the Marxist–Feminist Literature Collective, 'and their connection in literary history is almost as intimate as their etymology.'[77] But argument-from-etymology lost its status as a logical proof long ago, and you can no more prove that genre is intimately connected with gender because both words happen to derive from *genus* ('kind') than you can prove an affinity between Christians and cretins on the grounds of a common origin of those words in *christianus*. The investigation of what Kathleen Blake calls 'gender generics'[78] leads away from names and forms and into those exclusionist practices which, in the past, have obliged women to avail themselves of genres deemed marginal to an androcentric culture, and therefore non-canonical in status. In those centuries when English poetry was seen as an elaborately allusive gloss on various Greek and Latin exemplars, the denial of a classical education to women was bound to have the effect of making them feel somehow unqualified to write the 'learned' poetry preserved in a high-brow print-culture which dissociated itself from such 'vulgar' manifestations of oral culture as the ballad. It is therefore no mere coincidence that women were custodians of the ballad tradition in the crucial period when ballads were first collected and printed. The ballad singer with the oldest and most extensive repertoire was Anna Gordon, whose ballads are called 'stories of a woman's tradition' by David Buchan, and whose immediate sources were all women.[79] According to this construction of the evidence, ballads are old-wives' tales which were able to develop and change in authentically feminine ways mainly because men left them alone. Not until the eighteenth century, when they became the object of antiquarian curiosity, did ballads come under the scrutiny of men who saw it as their duty to 'correct' the transcripts which came their way so that the ballads would look more like publishable poems when they first appeared in print.

That situation cannot be paralleled exactly in a print-culture controlled by male publishers, although the relation of women writers to that most recent of traditional genres, the novel, is not entirely dissimilar. Novels developed as a 'low' form in the eighteenth century, and were not only easier to read than poetry but also suspiciously easy to write. 'There is no species of art which is so free from rigid requirements', George Eliot observed when trying to explain the proliferation of silly novels by lady novelists for lady readers.[80] To think of women as having a special aptitude for writing novels was therefore something of a back-handed compliment, given the low status of a product which, as Jane Austen complained, tended to be thought of as 'only a novel', and therefore as something to be taken no more seriously than women themselves.[81] 'Of all departments of literature, Fiction is the one to which, by nature and by circumstance, women are best adapted', wrote G. H. Lewes when surveying 'the lady novelists' in 1852. 'The domestic experiences which form the bulk of woman's knowledge finds an appropriate form in novels.'[82] With the connection between gender and genre posed in such condescending terms, spirited protests were called for, although few were as memorable as Olive Schreiner's mockery of the belief that 'there must be some inherent connection in the human brain between the ovarian sex function and the art of fiction'.[83]

None of those who spoke of the dubious aptitude which women were supposed to have for fiction in the nineteenth century ever considered that women might write novels for exactly the same reasons as men did, namely the hope of making a living by them (Elizabeth Gaskell and Frances Trollope supported families from their literary earnings), and a sense that the novel was the supreme modern form with the same kind of future and mass audience which films enjoy nowadays. The difficulty with trying to make the 'aptitude' case academically respectable by arguing (as Gilbert and Gubar do) that 'the English novel seems to have been in some sense a female invention'[84] is that it involves ignoring the male inventors who figure prominently in most non-feminist accounts of the rise of the novel: Defoe, Richardson, Fielding, Sterne and the rest. A stronger position to take when arguing that gender is the mutant gene in genre-development is to point to differences discernible when men and women work in the 'same' genre. An exemplary instance here is Ellen Moers' dissociation of a 'female gothic' style of fiction represented by Ann Radcliffe's *The mysteries of Udolpho* (1794) from what comes to be recognised consequently as a male gothic mode, that 'terror' gothic of which the founding texts are Horace Walpole's *The castle of Otranto* (1764) and M. G. Lewis' *The monk* (1796).[85] The two types share certain conventions: a location which is geographically and/or historically remote; mysterious happenings which elicit a spectrum of responses from curiosity to terror; the family machinery of wills and inheritances. But they differ in emphasis if only because women don't normally terrorise men in the way that men are capable of terrorising women. Female gothic offers women the vicarious experience of romantic release from a threatening entrapment. 'Women are cast as victims in a man's world', Kay Mussell explains in her survey of the genre, 'but through the demonstration of feminine virtues, the victim proves herself worthy of salvation through the love of the hero, who becomes her deliverer from the terrors that beset her.'[86] All such explanations of female gothic assume the existence of a psychological centre which controls the constitutive elements, although opinions vary as to what that centre might be. To Claire Kahane, for instance, it is 'the spectral presence of a dead–undead mother, archaic and all-encompassing, a ghost signifying the problematics of female identity which the heroine must confront'.[87] Much depends, therefore, on which female gothic text is taken as being prototypical; for Moers, it is Mary Shelley's *Frankenstein* (1818). But no matter which text gets favoured as a result of differing emphases within feminism itself, it is clearly preferable to have the female gothic isolated as a separate category than to have the texts which comprise it treated as inferior or decadent manifestations of a type of fiction for which the normative criteria are novels written by men. For once that demarcation has been made, it becomes possible to discern mutations within the female gothic as such, and to see how the 'sentimental' gothic of Radcliffe becomes the 'erotic' gothic in novels such as Rosemary Rogers' *Wicked, loving lies* (1976), which adds more or less explicit descriptions of more or less illicit sexual encounters to the familiar gothic mix of mystery, danger and romance.[88]

As with the feminist critique of language, the purpose of gender generics is to get certain forms which are believed to be gender-free recognised as gender-specific, which usually means male-specific. This can be done by a process of gender-reversal – imagining what a particular type of narrative would look like if the sexes of its leading characters were reversed. 'What if Bartleby were a woman?' asked Patricia Barber when thinking about Herman Melville's 'Bartleby the scrivener: a story of Wall Street' (1853). Her principal aim in transforming last century's male scrivener into this century's female typist was to reveal a repressed element in Melville's text, namely that it is 'essentially a love story, a story about a man who is confined in an office setting that forbids intimacy and who comes to love a person he cannot save'.[89] But the same exercise can be used to reveal the gendering of generic conventions. When Erica Jong read Fielding's *Tom Jones* (1749–50), she asked herself, 'What if Tom Jones had been a woman?' Her entertaining answer to that question is a gender-reversed picaresque novel called *Fanny* (1980), which reveals gender-discrimination by situating itself among a variety of eighteenth-century texts. These include John Cleland's pornographic *Fanny Hill* (1748–49) and that parody of Richardson's *Pamela* (1740) which Fielding called *Joseph Andrews* (1742), taking as his theme the sexual harassment of

Pamela's brother by Lady Booby, and treating gender-reversal —
revealingly — as a wholly comic device. In *Fanny* and similar
exercises — such as Rita Mae Brown's *Rubyfruit jungle* (1973), which
is a lesbian appropriation of the picaresque novel — what come under
attack are the limitations of traditional genres, and specifically the
way in which their exemplary texts are not only shaped by the
possibilities of exclusively masculine modes of experience but also
get talked about as if they were gender-free and purely aesthetic in
form.

Given the widespread preoccupation in the women's movement with
the cultural determinants of women's 'experience', a great deal of
interest has been shown in feminist transformations of the
Bildungsroman, which Goethe is usually credited with having invented
in *Wilhelm Meisters Lehrjahre* (1795–6) and Günter Grass with having
discredited in *The tin drum* (1959). But in so far as women react
differently from men to the acculturation processes of a male-
dominated society, their 'development' is likely to result in a degree of
alienation far removed from that sense of having come to terms with
society which is the destination of a successful *Bildung* in the masculine
tradition. A study of the 'female' *Bildungsroman* which includes
Dorothy Richardson's *Pilgrimage* (1915–38) and Simone de Beauvoir's
Memoirs of a dutiful daughter (1958) among its representative texts
notes that heroines are significantly absent from this genre in the
nineteenth century, because 'for the female heroine womanhood is
often the obstacle to her development' in a society which favours men;
and another study, this time of the 'feminist' *Bildungsroman*, where
the texts discussed include Lisa Alther's *Kinflicks* (1975) and Sheila
Ballantyne's *Norma Jean the termite queen* (1975), observes the
tendency to displace 'development' from a past into a future in which
heroines can be free from those male-determined roles which restrict
their possibilities of self-fulfilment in a male-dominated society.[90] The
sequence of events which brings success to the hero of a *Bildungsroman*
may bring disaster to the heroine of one, as can be seen by comparing
the status of sexual initiation in masculine and feminine versions of the
genre. 'Female *Bildung* tends to get stuck in the bedroom', Nancy K.
Miller observes.[91] The reason for this, she thinks, is that 'the novel,
more than any other form of art, is forced by the contract of the genre
to negotiate with social realities in order to remain legible' — and that
not until new plots are sanctioned for women in their everyday lives will
the female or feminist *Bildungsroman* be anything other than a record

of maladjustment to society, an anti-*Bildungsroman* in effect. Traditionally, our hero succeeds; but our heroine, if she is lucky, merely survives, which is why Linda Howe thinks that women's versions of the *Bildungsroman* such as Margaret Atwood's *Bodily harm* (1982) and Marge Piercy's *Braided lives* (1982) should be called 'narratives of survival'.[92]

v

As most of the writing taught in traditional courses of literary study was produced by men, the feminist critique which exposes its characteristic biases needs to be complemented by a gynocritics which proposes alternative texts for study. Before gradualists can draw up their supplementary syllabuses, however, or separatists their alternative ones, it is necessary to know just what there is to choose from. The groundwork of gynocritics is therefore archival and bibliographical, and results in the production of invaluable checklists, not only of unpublished materials but also of publications long since forgotten and not even mentioned in such standard reference works as the *Cambridge bibliography of English literature*.[93] The burgeoning of women's studies makes it feasible economically for feminist presses and reprint publishers to begin the task of promulgating this vast corpus of texts. Selections can then start to appear either in separatist anthologies of women's writing such as Mahl and Koon's *The female spectator* (1978), which presents some previously unpublished material written before 1800, or (on a much smaller scale) – and as a result of 'affirmative action' taken against non-feminist publishers – in anthologies which are used widely as set-texts in literature courses, such as the *Norton anthology of English poetry*, which before feminists intervened included only six women among its 175 poets.

The search for 'lost' women writers is conducted much more diligently but no less enthusiastically than the eighteenth-century search for those 'uneducated' poets of natural genius who were exemplified (uniquely, as it turned out) by Robert Burns. Gray's speculation that a 'mute, inglorious Milton' might be buried in the country churchyard he celebrated is paralleled by Olive Schreiner's lament for all those female Shakespeares who were condemned to lives of domestic choring and were thus 'stifled out without one line written'.[94] Their emblem, evoked by Virginia Woolf, is 'Shakespeare's sister', that imaginary woman who would never have had a chance to be Shakespeare because she was a woman.[95] 'Lost' is a problematic term in this context, for it covers three different phenomena: women who never wrote but might have done so if conditions had been more propitious (those mute Miltons who are logically impossible, since Milton had to write Milton's poems in order to become 'Milton'); women who wrote but never had anything published; and those who got into print but were forgotten sooner or later, whether they published anonymously ('Anon . . . was often a woman', Woolf reminds us),[96] or pseudonymously, or used their unmarried names or their married ones. 'Lost' also covers two quite distinct operations, one of which is accidental and the other deliberate. Feminists tend to favour the latter construction, agreeing with Annis V. Pratt that women writers were 'not haphazardly "forgotten" but deliberately buried', because until very recently the modes of production and circulation of books were entirely under the control of male gatekeepers of the publishing and reviewing networks.[97] The absence of women's writing from literary histories signals acts of erasure which betoken patriarchal conspiracy.

Although the content of such an argument is undeniably feminist, the form of it is not. It is to be encountered in any body of criticism which takes up the cause of some group which feels itself to be discriminated against; in the working-class version, for instance, weavers' ballads and Chartist novels are the excluded texts, and the victimising agent is middle-class privilege.[98] Rival explanations of why so many women writers have been forgotten need to be investigated, therefore, even though they are hardly likely to be popular with some feminists. I am thinking, for instance, of studies in the sociology of literary taste like those conducted by Robert Escarpit, who once calculated that ninety-nine per cent of all writers are forgotten twenty years after their work has been published.[99] Even more contentious as an alternative to the conspiracy theory is the evaluative argument which holds that many female authors are justifiably forgotten because they don't write well enough. Nina Baym, for example, having read her way through novels by and about women in America from 1820 to 1870 confessed that she had 'not unearthed a forgotten Jane Austen or George Eliot, or hit upon even one novel . . . to set alongside *The scarlet letter*'.[100] Similar standards were evidently in Helen Gardner's mind when, in the course of revising *The Oxford book of English verse* (which Sir Arthur Quiller-Couch had edited in 1901), she dropped nineteen of the twenty-three women poets included, and was praised for doing so by Germaine Greer on the grounds that 'women writers are not well served by the persistence of a critical double standard, which now threatens to survive as a hypocritical capitulation to militant feminist pressure, especially in universities'.[101]

However that kind of evaluative criticism was losing prestige when feminist criticism got under way. People who believe there are better things to do with literary texts than to rank them by allegedly absolute criteria turned to that relativistic 'interest' theory of value which predicts that different communities will value different things for different reasons, and that these factors will determine, among other things, which texts each community agrees to call literature. It therefore seemed unnecessary to ask, as Virginia Moore once did, which women writers are fit to rank with Homer, Virgil, Dante and Shakespeare (only Sappho, apparently).[102] Yet feminist criticism has certainly been troubled by the double standard which comes into play when women trained to look for formalist markers of value confront feminist texts whose power of appeal derives from other sources. Accounts of such contradictory experiences − '*Shirley* is an interminable, often boring novel, artificial in structure, stilted in manner; but as a treatment of the feminine situation, truly compelling' (Spacks) − clearly illustrate Jane Gallop's point that 'the feminist critic in her inheritance from both feminism and criticism lives the at once enabling and disabling tension of a difference within'.[103]

Problems of value arise not only in clashes between feminism and formalism but also within feminism itself, where the issues are more sharply political than aesthetic. The gynocritical recovery of 'lost' texts tends to be regarded as an indisputably worthwhile and therefore self-justifying activity, as if it were always an occasion for rejoicing when that which was lost is found again. Once the absent texts are restored, however, you have to decide what to do with them, especially with those which express reactionary views on current feminist issues. Barbauld's essay 'On female studies' (1811), for instance, causes Mahl and Koon some embarrassment (they fear it might be thought 'hopelessly out of date') because it states that even an educated woman should expect to become 'a wife, a mother, [and] a mistress of a family'.[104] It is one thing to feel outraged at Nathaniel Hawthorne for calling writers of domestic and sentimental novels in the 1850s a 'damned mob of scribbling women'; but it is another thing altogether to read in the period and discover, as Beverly Voloshin did, that the fiction of those feminine fifties is 'duplicitous' because those who wrote it made 'a career of showing women that their place is the home'.[105] Being a woman, being a writer, and being a feminist are evidently separable constructions, none of which entails an inalienable connection with the other two.

The recovery of 'lost' women writers whose works are said to constitute a female tradition raises the question of how literary history ought to be written. Separatists who believe that women need rooms of their own in order to produce a literature of their own see nothing odd in the idea of a history of women's literature. It is assumed, no doubt correctly, that the profile of such a history would almost certainly differ from that presented in literary textbooks because, as Gerda Lerner argues, 'the periods in which basic changes occur in society and which historians commonly regard as turning points, are not necessarily the same for men and women'.[106] The virtue of a separatist literary history would be its engendering of a valuable sense of the continuity of women's writing. By showing women writers who their 'foremothers' were, it would diminish that frightening sense of writing in isolation ('I look everywhere for grandmothers', Elizabeth Barrett Browning complained, 'and see none').[107] It would also challenge significantly the non-feminist view that the novels of Austen and Eliot and Woolf are merely intermittent aberrations from a predominantly male literary tradition. 'This is one of the ways,' Adrienne Rich observes, 'in which women's work and thinking has been made to seem sporadic, errant, orphaned of any tradition of its own.'[108] A separatist literary history would demonstrate that discontinuity from generation to generation is not a characteristic of women's writing but rather the product of androcentric discourses about it.

Anthologies which reprint poetry and prose written entirely by women in the course of several hundred years encourage the belief that there is indeed a tradition of women's writing which is best studied in isolation from what comes to be thought of consequently as an exclusively masculine tradition. To what extent do women have 'a literature of their own', to recall the title of Elaine Showalter's excellent study of British women novelists from Charlotte Brontë to Doris Lessing? Not much, it would appear, in terms of the text to which Showalter's title alludes: 'If women lived in a different country from men, and had never read any of their writings', said John Stuart Mill, 'they would have had a literature of their own.'[109] But such conditions, of course, have never existed, for men and women inhabit the same countries and read one another's writings habitually.

As a sampling of anthologies like Ann Stafford's *The women poets in English* (1972) shows, the mere removal of texts with male signatures attached to them does not guarantee the elimination of all masculine traces from the remaining poems signed with female names. When the first Queen Elizabeth takes up her pen to write a love poem she freezes and burns like any male Petrarchist; an elegant encomium of Henry Lawes by Katherine Philips might have been written by Edmund Waller; and *The rape of the lock* presides over Lady Mary Wortley Montagu's poem on a case of smallpox.[110] By and large, women write (as men do) in currently fashionable styles, more of which are associated with men than with women for historical reasons which feminists have now made clear. So although a history of women's literature is conceivable, whether it would be worth attempting is questionable. It would be perverse, for example, to discuss the female novel of sensibility in complete isolation from what non-feminist literary historians call the sentimental novel, exemplified by Henry Mackenzie's *The man of feeling* (1771) and Sterne's *The sentimental journey* (1768). Between them, these writers fabricated a rhetoric of the emotions which could be used, like Petrarchism, for serious or ironic purposes. The sentimental novel is therefore an important precursor against which the novel of sensibility defines itself, and it would be disabling to ignore it simply because men happen to have written what were historically the most influential examples of the genre. All texts are hooked into 'intertextual' relationships with one another. Although it is possible to separate gynotexts from androtexts for expository or pedagogic purposes, the benefits of doing so are not self-evident except to women who have no qualms about repeating exactly the same mistake for which they take male critics to task, namely an exclusive preoccupation with the writings of one sex.

The idea of a separatist literary history is sustained also in the new women's literature which appeared as a creative response to the feminist critique. That kind of reciprocity is common in the history of literary studies, because each dominant type of literary criticism since at least the time of John Dryden has taken as normative the characteristics of a particular style of writing. What results in more recent manifestations of this phenomenon is a number of books which are marked by a certain knowingness and directed at the academies in the expectation of bypassing the reading public and achieving instant recognition as university set-texts. The novels of John Barth, for instance, have always kept an eye on what goes on in graduate seminars on the theory of fiction, and have managed to keep abreast of shifts in critical fashion from the myth criticism of *Giles goat boy* (1966) to the post-structuralism of *Letters* (1979). So it is hardly surprising that the salvaging by feminist critics of a tradition of female-specific writing which deals with female-specific themes has encouraged and has been encouraged by new writings which draw on and develop such themes. A notable instance is Marilyn French's novel *The women's room* (1978), which makes its way through a series of episodes which in turn manage to cover most of the important issues raised by feminist discourse about the nature and quality of women's lives in contemporary American society. It is tailor-made for women's studies students who need to be confronted from time to time with relevant material presented rather more engagingly than the average textbook or scholarly article. If such books did not exist, it would be necessary to invent them.

The non-separatist or 'accommodationist' view is that it would be enough to rewrite traditional histories in order to take account of the women's writing hitherto excluded. The result would be a better balanced literary history than those written either before the feminist intervention or promised subsequently by that separatism which, in the opinion of Iris Murdoch, 'leads to rubbish like "black studies" and "women's studies" '.[111] Both the separatist and accommodationist projects are made difficult, however, by a suspicion (originating outside of feminism) that the writing of literary history has become so difficult as to be impossible. Nobody is sure any longer what is and is not 'literature', and even if that were not the case there would still be uncertainty as to what might be said to constitute a history of it. To people who would like to see literary studies absorbed into the more comprehensive field of cultural studies, the concept of a literary tradition is already hopelessly idealist. It first demarcates an arbitrary category called 'the literary' from other cultural phenomena for which a marxist would expect to find common materialist explanations; and it then assumes that instances of it constitute a continuum on which literary historians are free to project those tripartite structures of development they are so fond of, such as birth–maturity–decline. Showalter's tripartite scheme, for instance, distinguishes a submissively 'feminine' stage of writing (1840–80) from a suffragist 'feminist' stage (1880–1920) preceding that 'female' one which began in 1920 and was revitalised in the 1960s.[112] As an expository device it has its uses, but as an idealist construct it is vulnerable to Juliet

Mitchell's objection: 'The female tradition in fiction is permeated by the specific social and sexual experiences of women but it does not constitute a subcultural art form in itself.'[113]

Another complicating factor for separatists who think of the female tradition somewhat simplistically as standing in opposition to the male tradition is that neither of these entities is a uniform construct. In androcentric criticism, 'tradition' evokes a variety of different usages: the imperial tradition which T. S. Eliot recognised in Virgil and Dante is different from the working-class tradition which F. R. Leavis admired Lawrence for understanding, and different again from that occult tradition which Kathleen Raine traces in Blake and Yeats. Harold Bloom, whose Freudian fathers-and-sons theory of literary influence is modified by Gilbert and Gubar in order to explain the dynamics of that 'great tradition of literature by women' which they trace in *The madwoman in the attic* (1979), favours a modified version of the nineteenth-century Romantic tradition. Each focuses on male writers, but none could be considered unequivocally representative of 'the male tradition'.[114]

As for 'the female tradition', that too is far from being a unitary concept, not only on account of political disagreements which situate women at different points along a spectrum which is feminist at one end and non-feminist at the other, but also because of sexual differences between lesbian and non-lesbian women. Significantly, lesbian attacks on the kind of writing promoted by gynocritics recapitulate the feminist attack on androcentric criticism. Bonnie Zimmerman, for instance, finds advocates of women's literature 'homophobic' in their preference for the work of heterosexual women.[115] Yet to a 'woman identified woman', lesbian texts such as Monique Wittig's — 'written by women exclusively for women, careless of male approval' — are exemplary in their 'total rupture with masculine culture'.[116] Lesbian writers find themselves oppressed therefore not only by the sexism of men but also by the 'heterosexism' of other women. Lesbian texts are omitted from feminist anthologies, and there is an inexplicable silence about lesbian writers in major critical studies published by Showalter, Moers, Spacks, Gilbert and Gubar: lesbian writing, it is said, has not been simply forgotten but deliberately 'erased'. Like the feminist criticism described in this book, lesbian feminism operates on two fronts. There is a 'lesbian critique' which undertakes the negative task of unmasking homophobia in feminist criticism; and there is also a contrastingly positive but unnamed activity which is 'concerned with the development of a uniquely lesbian perspective'. Jane Rule's *Lesbian images* (Garden City, NY, 1975) outlines a twentieth-century tradition of lesbian writing ignored by heterosexual feminists who, given their own struggle against the exclusionist practices of male literary historians, ought to know better.

All the evidence suggests that a tradition is made, not given: it is created retrospectively for self-validating purposes out of the present needs of a particular group of people, and is not handed down to everybody indiscriminately as a 'natural' inheritance. Each tradition is conceived of separately, and together they constitute a plurality. 'There is no single female tradition in literature', Moers reminds us.[117] They intersect with one another not only because different groups kidnap the same authors for different traditions (who now 'owns' the writings of Jane Austen, for instance?), but also because the same people find themselves affiliated to different groups for different reasons. It is only too easy to invent a tradition in which to place oneself and a few friends; but it is the quickest way of marginalising one's activities, or rather, of getting them designated marginal by outsiders. It would be a pity if the feminist critique, which has been so successful in identifying androcentric bias against women writers and in making possible a critical discourse free of such prejudices, should be betrayed by a gynocritics developed along separatist lines. For that would simply reproduce the polarity between women's writing and men's which feminist criticism set out to combat in the first place. And it would also make it that much harder next time to persuade men and women that they have far too much to learn from one another to risk going their separate ways.

Notes

1 The gendering of critical discourse

1 Cf. Laura Mulvey, 'Visual pleasure and narrative cinema', *Screen*, 16 (Autumn 1975), 6–18; E. Ann Kaplan, *Women and film: both sides of the camera* (London, 1983).

2 Daly, *Beyond God the father* (Boston, 1973), p. 47.

3 Cf. Christopher Norris, *Deconstruction: theory and practice* (London, 1982); Jonathan Culler, *On deconstruction* (Ithaca, 1982).

4 Gallop, *Feminism and psychoanalysis: the daughter's seduction* (London, 1982), p. xiii; on 'knowledge-as-rape' see Michèle Le Doeuff, 'Operative philosophy', *I&C*, no. 6 (Autumn 1979), 50–5.

5 Dworkin, *Our blood* (1976; London, 1982), pp. 61–2.

6 Morgan, 'Feminism and literary study', *Critical inquiry*, 2 (1976), 815, 809.

7 McConnell-Ginet, 'Linguistics and the feminist challenge', *Women and language in literature and society*, ed. Sally McConnell-Ginet *et al.* (New York, 1980), p. 16.

8 Terry Eagleton, *The rape of Clarissa* (Oxford, 1982), p. viii.

9 Shaw, 'Woman – man in petticoats [1927]', *Platform and pulpit*, ed. Dan H. Laurence (New York, 1961), p. 174.

10 Fetterley, *The resisting reader* (Bloomington, 1978), pp. 152–3, xvii.

11 Aiken, 'Scripture and poetic discourse in *The subjection of women*', *PMLA*, 98 (1983), 367.

12 Rowland, 'Women's studies courses', *Women's studies international forum*, 5 (1982), 493.

13 Black and Coward, 'Linguistic, social and sexual relations', *Screen education*, no. 39 (Summer 1981), 69–85; cf. Kate McKluskie, 'Women's language and literature: a problem in women's studies', *Feminist review*, no. 14 (June 1983), 51–61.

14 Spender, *Women of ideas and what men have done to them* (London, 1982), p. 531.

15 Coward, ' "This novel changes lives": are women's novels feminist novels?' *Feminist review*, no. 5 (1980), 55.

16 Perkins, 'Presidential address 1979: *E pluribus unum*', *PMLA*, 95 (1980), 314; cf. Joan Kelly, 'Early feminist theory and the *querelle des femmes*, 1400–1789', *Signs*, 8 (1982), 4–28, and the response by Susan Schibanoff, *Signs*, 9 (1983), 320–6.

17 Dinnage, 'Re-creating Eve', *New York review of books*, 20 December 1979, p. 6.

18 Todd, 'Women's fiction', *Times higher education supplement*, 24 December 1982, p. 15.

19 Cf. Margaret Lenta, 'Comedy, tragedy and feminism: the novels of

Richardson and Fielding', *English studies in Africa*, 26 (1983), 13–25.

20 Davis, *Women, race & class* (New York, 1981); Hull, 'Afro-American women poets: a bio-critical survey', *Shakespeare's sisters*, ed. Sandra M. Gilbert and Susan Gubar (Bloomington, 1979), p. 165; cf. Barbara Smith, 'Toward a black feminist criticism', *Women's studies international quarterly*, 2 (1979), 183–94; and Elly Bulkin's untitled contribution to 'An interchange on feminist criticism', *Feminist studies*, 8 (1982), 635–54.

21 Cf. Hélène Vivienne Wenzel, 'The text as body/politics: an appreciation of Monique Wittig's writings in context', *Feminist studies*, 7 (1981), 271.

22 *Psych et po* stands for *Psychanalyse et politique*: cf. Anna Gibbs, 'An alternative viewpoint', *Hecate*, 6 (1980), 34; Carolyn Greenstein Burke, 'Report from Paris: women's writing and the women's movement', *Signs*, 3 (1978), 846; Alice Jardine, 'Gynesis', *Diacritics*, 12 (Summer 1982), 54–65.

23 Cixous, 'The laugh of the Medusa', *Signs*, 1 (1967), 883.

24 Cf. Carole Ferrier, 'Writing the history of women's writing', *Hecate*, 8 (1982), 80.

25 *New French feminisms*, ed. Elaine Marks and Isabelle de Courtivron (1980; Brighton, 1981); cf. Meaghan Morris, 'Aspects of current French feminist literary criticism', *Hecate*, 5 (1979), 63–72; Alice Jardine, 'Pretexts for the transatlantic feminist', *Yale French studies*, no. 62 (1981), 220–36; Ailbhe Smyth, 'Contemporary French feminism: an annotated shortlist of recent works', *Hecate*, 9 (1983), 203–36.

26 Stimpson, 'On feminist criticism', *What is criticism?*, ed. Paul Hernadi (Bloomington, 1981), p. 230.

2 Constructing feminist theories of criticism

1   Lerner, 'Placing women in history: a 1975 perspective', *Liberating women's history*, ed. Berenice A. Carroll (Urbana, 1976), p. 365.

2   Pratt, 'The new feminist criticisms: exploring the history of the new space', *Beyond intellectual sexism*, ed. Joan I. Roberts (New York, 1976), p. 187; Daly, *Gyn/ecology* (1978; London, 1979), p. 23.

3   Evans, 'In praise of theory: the case for Women's Studies', *Theories of women's studies*, ed. Gloria Bowles and Renate Duelli Klein (London, 1983), p. 224.

4   Barthes, 'Writers, intellectuals, teachers [1971]', *Image–music–text* (Glasgow, 1977), p. 201.

5   McMillan, *Women, reason and nature* (Oxford, 1982), p. 119.

6   Cf. Judith Hole and Ellen Levine, *Rebirth of feminism* (New York, 1971), p. 110.

7   Morgan, 'Goodbye to all that [1970]', *The American sisterhood*, ed. Wendy Martin (New York, 1972), p. 367.

8   Stead, *Seven poor men of Sydney* (1934; London, 1965), p. 205.

9   Cf. Hole and Levine, *Rebirth of feminism*, p. 442.

10 Beauvoir, *Force of circumstance* (1963; London, 1965), p. 192; for her later view that 'the emancipation of women must be the work of women

themselves' see Alice Jardine, 'Interview with Simone de Beauvoir [1977]', *Signs*, 5 (1979), 235.

11 Delaney, 'Confessions of an ex-handkerchief head; or why I am not a feminist', *Queen's quarterly*, 89 (1982), 824.

12 Hartmann, 'Summary and response', *Women and revolution*, ed. Lydia Sargent (London, 1981), p. 364.

13 Marxist–Feminist Literature Collective (cited subsequently as 'M–FLC'), 'Women's writing: *Jane Eyre, Shirley, Villette, Aurora Leigh*', *I&C*, no. 3 (1978), 27–48.

14 Taylor, 'Class and gender in Charlotte Brontë's *Shirley*', *Feminist review*, no. 1 (1979), 92.

15 Engels, *The origin of the family, private property and the state* (London, 1940), p. 69.

16 Strindberg, *Miss Julie* (London, 1964), p. 26.

17 Beauvoir interviewed by Alice Schwarzer (1972), *New French feminisms*, ed. Marks and de Courtivron, p. 146.

18 Mill, *The subjection of women* (London, 1869), p. 57.

19 *The poetical works of Elizabeth Barrett Browning* (London, 1897), pp. 287–90.

20 Campbell, 'A feminist sexual politics: now you see it, now you don't', *Feminist review*, no. 5 (1981), 15; Summers, *Damned whores and God's police* (Ringwood, Victoria, 1975), pp. 198–9; Burris, 'The Fourth World manifesto [1971]', *Radical feminism*, ed. Anne Koedt *et al.* (New York, 1973), pp. 322–57.

21 Marx, 'Theses on Feuerbach, XI', *The German ideology* (1846; London, 1970), p. 123.

22 Dworkin, *Our blood*, p. 9.

23 Fetterley, *Resisting reader*, p. viii.

24 Robinson, 'Dwelling in decencies [1971]', *Sex, class, and culture* (Bloomington, 1978), pp. 19–20.

25 Cf. Georg Lukács, *Studies in European realism* (London, 1950), p. 9.

26 Macherey, *A theory of literary production* (1966; London, 1978); Eagleton, *Criticism and ideology* (London, 1976).

27 Boumelha, *Thomas Hardy and women* (Brighton, 1982), p. 5; cf. Mary Childers, 'Thomas Hardy, the man who "liked" women', *Criticism*, 23 (1981), 317–34.

28 Adorno, *Prisms* (1967; Cambridge, Mass., 1981), p. 32.

29 Poovey, '*Persuasion* and the promises of love', *The representation of women in fiction*, ed. Carolyn G. Heilbrun and Margaret Higonnet (Baltimore, 1983), p. 176.

30 Dworkin, *Our blood*, p. 7; Spender, *Women of ideas*, p. xi.

31 Friedan, *The feminine mystique* (London, 1963); *The second stage* (New York, 1981), p. 313; cf. Judith Stacey, 'The new conservative feminism', *Feminist studies*, 9 (1983), 559–83; Andrea Dworkin, *Right-wing women* (New York, 1983).

32 Rodney Wetherell, 'Interview with Christina Stead', *Australian literary studies*, 9 (1980), 439; Lessing, *The golden notebook* (1962; London, 1973), p. 9.

33 K. A. McKenzie, *Edith Simcox and George Eliot* (London, 1961), p. 97; cf. Zelda Austen, 'Why feminist critics are angry with George Eliot', *College English*, 37 (1976), 549–61.

34 Millett, *Sexual politics*, p. 139.

35 *Shakespeare's sisters*, ed. Gilbert and Gubar, p. xxiii.

36 Williams, *Marxism and literature* (London, 1977), p. 110; Gramsci, *Selections from the prison notebooks* (1965; London, 1971), pp. 12–13.

37 Ricoeur, *Freud and philosophy* (New Haven, 1970), pp. 32–6.

38 Eagleton, 'The idealism of American criticism', *New left review*, no. 27 (1981), 65.

39 Saunders, 'Signing on: the currency of semiotics', *Age monthly review* (Melbourne), 3 (May 1983), 4; cf. Elizabeth Cowie, ' "Woman as sign" ', *m/f*, no. 1 (1978), 49–63; Cathy Schwichtenberg, 'Erotica: the semey side of semiotics', *Sub-stance*, no. 32 (1981), 26–38; Kaja Silverman, *The subject of semiotics* (London, 1984).

40 *The female spectator*, ed. Mary R. Mahl and Helene Koon (Bloomington, 1977).

41 Saussure, *Course in general linguistics*, p. 120.

42 See Ian Maclean, *The Renaissance notion of woman* (Cambridge, 1980), pp. 2–3.

43 Felman, 'Woman and madness: the critical phallacy', *Diacritics*, 5 (Winter 1975), 3.

44 Beauvoir, *The second sex* (1949; London, 1953), p. 16.

45 Meredith, *The egoist* (1879; Harmondsworth, 1968), p. 76.

46 Donovan, 'Beyond the net: feminist criticism as a moral criticism', *Denver quarterly*, 17 (1983), 50.

47 Showalter, 'Towards a feminist poetics', *Women writing and writing about women*, ed. Mary Jacobus (London, 1979), p. 39.

48 Trilling, *The opposing self* (1955; Oxford, 1980), p. [xii].

49 Cf. Hans Robert Jauss, 'An introduction to the hermeneutic concept of alterity', *New literary history*, 10 (1979), 187–91.

50 Bamber, *Comic women, tragic men* (Stanford, 1982), pp. 42, 5.

51 Maclean, *Renaissance notion of woman*, p. 12.

52 I Corinthians 11.3; Freud, 'Femininity', *New introductory lectures on psycho-analysis* (1932; London, 1964), pp. 125–9.

53 Makin quoted from *Female spectator*, ed. Mahl and Koon, p. 126.

54 Beauvoir, *Second sex*, p. 273; cf. Anne Dickason, 'The feminine as universal', *Feminism and philosophy*, ed. Mary Vetterling-Braggin *et al.* (Totowa, NJ, 1977), pp. 79–100.

55 Ortner, 'Is female to male as nature is to culture?' *Women, culture, and society*, ed. Michelle Zimbalist Rosaldo and Louise Lamphere (Stanford, 1974), pp. 67–87; cf. Penelope Brown and L. J. Jordanova, 'Oppressive dichotomies: the nature/culture debate', *Women in society* (London, 1981), pp. 224–41.

56 Lévi-Strauss, *Structural anthropology* (1958; New York, 1963), p. 61.

57 *New French feminisms*, ed. Marks and de Courtivron, p. 36.

58 Figes, *Patriarchal attitudes* (1970; London, 1978), p. 26.

59 Cf. Maren Lockwood, *The new feminist movement* (New York, 1974),

pp. 214–15; Natalie Zemon Davis, 'Women on top', *The reversible world*, ed. Barbara A. Babcock (Ithaca, 1978), pp. 147–90.

60   Daly, *Gyn/ecology*, p. 155.

61   Laurence, *This side Jordan* (1960; Toronto, 1976), pp. 232–3; Doyle, *Round the red lamp* (1894; London, 1903), pp. 127–8.

62   Spivak, 'French feminism in an international frame', *Yale French studies,* no. 62 (1981), 183.

63   Cf. Freud, *Three essays on the theory of sexuality* (1905; London, 1949), p. 221; Koedt, 'The myth of the vaginal orgasm [1968]', *Radical feminism*, ed. Koedt, pp. 198–207.

64   Scholes, *Semiotics and interpretation* (New Haven, 1982), p. 136; Alice Kahn Ladas *et al.*, *The G spot* (New York, 1982).

65   D. H. Lawrence, *Lady Chatterley's lover* (1928; Harmondsworth, 1960), pp. 232, 210; Scholes, *Semiotics and interpretation*, p. 140.

66   Schor, 'Female paranoia: the case for psychoanalytic feminist criticism', *Yale French studies*, no. 62 (1981), 214, 216.

67   Klaus, 'Women in the mirror: using novels to study Victorian women', *The women of England from Anglo-Saxon times to the present*, ed. Barbara Kanner (Hamden, 1979), pp. 320–1.

68   Laslett, 'The wrong way through the telescope: a note on literary evidence in sociology and in historical sociology', *British journal of sociology*, 27 (1976), 333, 328; but cf. Judith Laurence-Anderson, 'Changing affective life in eighteenth-century England and Samuel Richardson's *Pamela*', *Studies in eighteenth-century culture*, 10 (1981), 445–56.

69   *What manner of woman*, ed. Springer (New York, 1977), p. xv.

70   Marcus, 'Liberty, sorority, misogyny', *Representation of women in fiction*, ed. Heilbrun and Higonnet, p. 63.

71   M–FLC, 'Women's writing', p. 27.

72   Ward, *Pure sociology* (New York, 1903), p. 292.

73   Woolf, *Three guineas* (London, 1938), p. 265; Wilden, 'The critique of phallocentrism: Daniel Paul Schreber on women's liberation', *System and structure* (London, 1972), pp. 278–301.

74   Derrida, 'Structure, sign, and play in the discourse of the human sciences [1966]', *The languages of criticism and the sciences of man: the structuralist controversy*, ed. Richard Macksey and Eugenio Donato (Baltimore, 1970), p. 248.

75   Derrida, *Of grammatology* (1967; Baltimore, 1976), p. 128.

76   Derrida, 'Structure, sign, and play', p. 265.

77   Lacan, *The language of the self* (1956; Baltimore, 1968), p. 187; cf. John Forrester, 'Philology and the phallus', *The talking cure*, ed. Colin MacCabe (London, 1981), pp. 56–7.

78   Gallop, *Feminism and psychoanalysis*, p. 98.

79   Moers, *Literary women*, p. 169; cf. Stephen Heath, 'Difference', *Screen*, 19 (Autumn 1978), 54–5.

80   Gallop, 'Phallus/penis: same difference', *Men by women*, ed. Janet Todd (New York, 1981), p. 244.

81   Jones, 'The early development of female sexuality', *International journal of psychoanalysis*, 8 (1927), 459.

82 Mitchell, *Psychoanalysis and feminism* (1974; Harmondsworth, 1975), p. xv; Jacques Lacan, *Feminine sexuality,* ed. Juliet Mitchell and Jacqueline Rose (London, 1982), p. 23.

83 Rose, 'The radical who reclaimed Freud', *Times higher education supplement*, 2 October 1981, p. 12.

84 Derrida (1973) quoted by Culler, *On deconstruction*, p. 172; cf. Derrida, 'The purveyor of truth', *Yale French studies*, no. 52 (1975), 95–7. In a 1981 exchange with Derrida, Christie V. McDonald glosses 'phallogocentrism' as 'the complicity of Western metaphysics with a notion of male firstness' ('Choreographies', *Diacritics*, 12 [Summer 1982], 69).

85 Cixous, 'Sorties [1975]', *New French feminisms*, ed. Marks and de Courtivron, pp. 92–3; Austen, *Persuasion* (1818; Oxford, 1923), p. 234.

86 Donoghue, *Ferocious alphabets* (London, 1981), pp. 98–9, 152–3.

87 Norris, *Deconstruction*, p. 31; cf. Frances Bartkowski, 'Feminism and deconstruction: "a union forever deferred" ', *enclitic*, 4 (Fall 1980), 70–7.

88 Féral, 'Antigone or *The irony of the tribe*', *Diacritics*, 8 (Fall 1978), 6–7.

89 Adler, 'Method and madness in female writing [II]', *Hecate*, 7 (1981), 28.

90 Johnson, *The critical difference* (Baltimore, 1980), pp. 5, 12.

91 Sandra M. Gilbert and Susan Gubar, *The madwoman in the attic* (New Haven, 1979), p. 3; Joyce, *Finnegans wake* (1939; London, 1950), p. 560.

92 Cf. Sheila Ryan Johansson, ' "Herstory" as history: new field or another fad?' *Liberating women's history*, ed. Carroll, pp. 400–30.

93 Stefan Kanfer, 'Sispeak: a msguided attempt to change herstory', *Time*, 23 October 1972, p. 45.

94 Marcuse, *One dimensional man* (London, 1964), p. 11.

3 Dismantling androcentric assumptions

1 Beckett, *The unnamable* (1958; New York, 1970), p. 139.

2 Black and Coward, 'Linguistic, social and sexual relations', p. 78; cf. Dale Spender, *Man made language* (London, 1980); Nancy Ritchie Key, *Male/female language* (Metuchen, NJ, 1975).

3 Richardson, *The tunnel* (1919), rpt. *Pilgrimage* (4 vols., London, 1938), vol. 2, p. 210.

4 Hardy, *Far from the madding crowd* (1874; London, 1912), p. 415.

5 *Adrienne Rich's poetry*, ed. Barbara Charlesworth Gelpi and Albert Gelpi (New York, 1975), pp. 48, 50; Varda One, *Manglish* (Venice, Calif., 1970).

6 Gillman, 'The looking-glass through Alice', *Gender and literary voice*, ed. Janet Todd (New York, 1980), p. 12.

7 Gilbert and Gubar, *Madwoman in the attic*, p. 31.

8 Jacobus, 'The difference of view', *Women writing*, ed. Jacobus, p. 19.

9 Kaplan, 'Speaking/writing/feminism', *On gender and writing*, ed. Michelene Wandor (London, 1983), p. 58.

10 Wittig, *The lesbian body* (1973; London, 1975), pp. 10–11; cf. Namascar Shaktini, 'Displacing the phallic subject: Wittig's lesbian writing', *Signs*, 8 (1982), 29–44.

11 Jacques Lacan, *Écrits: a selection* (1966; London, 1977); 'French Freud', *Yale French studies*, no. 48 (1972).

12 Kristeva (1974) quoted by Heath, 'Difference', p. 81.

13 Cf. Casey Miller and Kate Swift, *Words and women* (London, 1977), p. 117.

14 Bodine, 'Androcentrism in prescriptive grammar', *Language in society*, 4 (1975), 129–46; cf. Elizabeth S. Sklar, 'Sexist grammar revisited', *College English*, 45 (1983), 348–58.

15 Black and Coward, 'Linguistic, social and sexual relations', p. 85.

16 Twain, *A tramp abroad* (London, 1880), p. 543; cf. Fodor István, 'The origin of grammatical gender', *Lingua*, 8 (1959), 1–41, 186–214; Marielouise Janssen-Jurreit, 'The genitals of speech', *Sexism* (1976; London, 1982), pp. 290–8.

17 Carew, 'An elegie upon the death of Dr John Donne [1633]', *The metaphysical poets*, ed. Helen Gardner (Harmondsworth, 1957), p. 142.

18 Strainchamps, 'Our sexist language', *Woman in sexist society*, ed. Vivian Gornick and Barbara K. Moran (New York, 1971), p. 241.

19 Cf. Una Stannard, *Mrs Man* (San Francisco, 1977).

20 Miller and Swift, *The handbook of non-sexist writing* (1980; London, 1981), p. 88.

21 Spenser, *The faerie queene*, V ii 30; *The Oxford dictionary of English proverbs*, 3rd edn (Oxford, 1970), p. 758; P. Price, 'Violation (Biafra)', *Mother I'm rooted*, ed. Kate Jennings (Melbourne, 1975), p. 431.

22 'Adamless Eden' was the name of Mary Walker's projected colony for young women in the 1890s: see Nina Auerbach, *Communities of women* (Cambridge, Mass., 1978), pp. 28–30; cf. Barbara Hill Rigney, *Lilith's daughters* (Madison, 1982), p. 75.

23 Cf. Pamela Howard, 'Watch your language, men', *More*, 2 (February 1972), 3–4.

24 'Mhysteria' in *Women and literature*, 7 (1979), 42; 'misstery' in *Diacritics*, 7 (Summer 1977), 70; Pauline Bart (1974), quoted in *Doing feminist research*, ed. Helen Roberts (London, 1981), p. 22.

25 Gearhart, *The wanderground* (Watertown, Mass., 1979), pp. 15, 12.

26 Daly, *Gyn/ecology*, pp. 4, xi, 24; for the argument 'that Daly pursues a politics of subverting isolated signs, not discourses' see Meaghan Morris, 'A-mazing grace: notes on Mary Daly's poetics', *Lip*, no. 7 (1982/3), 32.

27 Carter, 'The language of sisterhood', *The state of the language*, ed. Leonard Michaels and Christopher Ricks (Berkeley, 1980), p. 233.

28 Cf. Randolph Quirk and Janet Whitcut, 'Lingo', *Times educational supplement*, 2 May 1980, p. 21.

29 Wise and Rafferty, 'Sex bias and language', *Sex roles*, 8 (1982), 1195.

30 Cf. John T. Gage, 'Philosophies of style and their implications for composition', *College English*, 41 (1980), 617.

31 Dillon, 'Whorfian stylistics', *Journal of literary semantics*, 11 (1982), 75, 76.

32 Frye, *Anatomy of criticism* (Princeton, 1957); C. G. Jung, 'Psychology and literature [1930]', *The spirit in man, art and literature* (New York, 1966); cf. Annis Pratt, *Archetypal patterns in women's fiction* (Brighton, 1982).

33 Cf. David Lodge, 'Where it's at: the poetry of psychobabble [1980]', *Working with structuralism* (London, 1981), pp. 188–96.

34 Mitchell, *Woman's estate* (Harmondsworth, 1971), p. 61; cf. *Ms* magazine, 'A guide to consciousness-raising [1972]', *Women's liberation in the twentieth century*, ed. Mary C. Lynn (New York, 1975), pp. 111–18.

35 Ferguson quoted by Cheri Register, 'American feminist literary criticism: a bibliographical introduction', *Feminist literary criticism*, ed. Josephine Donovan (Lexington, 1975), p. 7; Bartky, 'Toward a phenomenology of feminist consciousness [1975]', *Feminism and philosophy*, ed. Vetterling-Braggin, p. 26.

36 Spacks, *The female imagination* (1975; New York, 1976), p. 197.

37 Rowland, 'Women's studies courses', p. 494.

38 Dolores Barracaro Schmidt, 'The great American bitch', *College English*, 32 (1971), 904; cf. Cynthia Griffin Wolff, 'A mirror for men: stereotypes of women in literature', *Massachusetts review*, 13 (1972), 205–18.

39 Woolf, 'Professions for women [1942], *Collected essays* (4 vols., London, 1966/7), vol. 2, p. 286; *The poems of Coventry Patmore*, ed. Frederick Page (London, 1949), p. 111.

40 Mary Carruthers, 'Imagining women: notes towards a feminist poetic', *Massachusetts review*, 20 (1979), 383.

41 *Medieval English lyrics*, ed. R. T. Davies (London, 1963), no. 174 (15th century).

42 Register, 'American feminist literary criticism', p. 20 (quoting Wendy Martin).

43 Mailer, *The prisoner of sex* (Boston and Toronto, 1971).

44 Franklin, 'Traditional literary study – in the subjunctive mood', *Female studies VI*, ed. Nancy Hoffman *et al.* (1972; New York, 1973), p. 44.

45 Arthur, 'Women and the family in ancient Greece', *Yale review*, 71 (1982), 535.

46 Showalter, *A literature of their own* (1977; London, 1978), p. 315.

47 Robinson, *Sex, class, and culture*, p. 51.

48 Auerbach, *Woman and the demon* (Cambridge, Mass., 1982), pp. 2, 185.

49 Curtius, *European literature and the Latin middle ages* (1948; London, 1953).

50 Lieberman, 'Sexism and the double standard in literature', *Images of women in fiction*, ed. Susan Koppelman Cornillon (Bowling Green, 1972), p. 328.

51 Kennard, *Victims of convention* (Hamden, 1978).

52 'A pastoral letter to New England's churches', Judith Papachristou, *Women together* (New York, 1976), p. 12; cf. Peter Demetz, 'The elm

and the vine: notes toward the history of a marriage topos', *PMLA*, 73 (1958), 521–32.

53 Farwell, 'Feminist criticism and the concept of the poetic persona', *Women, literature, criticism*, ed. Harry R. Garvin (Lewisberg, 1978), p. 144.

54 Rukeyser, 'The poem as mask [1971]', *No more masks*, ed. Florence Howe and Ellen Bass (Garden City, NY, 1973), p. [1].

55 Farwell, 'Feminist criticism', p. 153.

56 Fauchrey quoted by Nancy K. Miller, *The heroine's text* (New York, 1980), pp. 153–4.

57 Firestone, *The dialectic of sex* (1971; London, 1972), p. 121.

58 Basch, *Relative creatures* (London, 1974), pp. 35–6.

59 Gilman, *The man-made world* (London, 1911), p. 91; cf. Naomi Weisstein, ' "Kinde[r], Kuche, Kirche" as scientific law: psychology constructs the female [1968]', *Sisterhood is powerful*, ed. Robin Morgan (New York, 1970), pp. 228–45.

60 Rowe, 'Feminism and fairy tales', *Women's studies*, 6 (1979), 239; Lieberman, ' "Some day my prince will come": female acculturation through the fairy tale', *College English*, 34 (1972), 395, 383; cf. Jennifer Waelti-Walters, 'On princesses: fairy tales, sex roles and loss of self', *International journal of women's studies*, 2 (1979), 180–8.

61 Sexton, *Transformations* (Boston, 1971), p. 1.

62 Cf. G. E. Larocque, 'You gotta kiss a lotta frogs before you find Prince Charming', *English journal*, 68 (December 1979), 31–5.

63 Atwood, 'The pleasures of rereading: a symposium', *New York Times Book Review*, 12 June 1983, p. 43.

64 Heilbrun, *Reinventing womanhood* (New York, 1979), p. 150.

65 Walsh, 'The devil and the deep blue sea', *New statesman*, 26 November 1980, p. 65.

66 Avery, 'Guardians of education', *London review of books*, 17 July to 6 August 1980, p. 23; Ferrier, 'Is an "images of woman" methodology adequate for reading Elizabeth Harrower's *The watch tower?*' *Who is she?*, ed. Shirley Walker (St Lucia, Queensland, 1983), p. 194.

67 Lanier, *The poems of Shakespeare's dark lady*, intro. A. L. Rowse (London, 1979), p. 78.

68 Rogers, *The troublesome helpmate* (Seattle, 1966), p. 11.

69 Tertullian quoted by Beauvoir, *Second sex*, pp. 184–5.

70 Weininger (1906) quoted by Hilary Simpson, *D. H. Lawrence and feminism* (London, 1982), pp. 90–1.

71 Kelso, *Doctrine for the lady of the Renaissance* (Urbana, 1956), p. 12.

72 Rogers, *Troublesome helpmate*, pp. 71, 76.

73 Letter written *c.* 1600 quoted by Evelyn M. Simpson, *A study of the prose works of John Donne* (Oxford, 1924), p. 298.

74 Maclean, *Renaissance notion of woman*, p. 85.

75 Cf. Lesley Johnson, 'Women on top: antifeminism in the fabliaux?' *Modern language review*, 78 (1983), 298–307.

76 Camden, *The Elizabethan woman* (London, 1952), pp. 241–3, 267.

77 *The works of Geoffrey Chaucer*, ed. F. N. Robinson, 2nd edn (London, 1957), p. 82.
78 Sontag, 'The pornographic imagination [1967]', *Styles of radical will* (New York, 1969), pp. 44, 57, 60, 70.
79 Dworkin, *Woman hating* (New York, 1974), p. 56.
80 Cf. Rosalind Innes, ' "What she needs is a good fuck" – rape and femininity', *Hecate*, 2 (July 1976), 23–30.
81 LaBelle, 'The propaganda of misogyny [1978]', *Take back the night*, ed. Laura Lederer (1980; New York, 1982), p. 172; Morgan, 'Theory and practice: pornography and rape [1977]', *ibid.*, p. 131.
82 Griffin, *Pornography and silence* (New York, 1981), p. 256.
83 Steinem, 'Erotica and pornography: a clear and present difference [1978]', *Take back the night*, ed. Lederer, p. 24; Carter, *The Sadeian woman* (London, 1979), p. 17.
84 Carter, *Sadeian woman*, p. 27.
85 Barrowclough, ' "Not a love story" ', *Screen*, 23 (November/December 1982), 32, 30.
86 G. Legman, *Rationale of the dirty joke* (1968; London, 1969), p. 549.
87 Stern, 'The body as evidence: a critical review of the pornography problematic', *Screen*, 23 (November/December 1982), 60; cf. Karen Jaehne, 'Confessions of a feminist porn programmer', *Film quarterly*, 37 (Fall 1983), 9–16.
88 Gilbert, 'Patriarchal poetry and women readers: reflections on Milton's bogey [1978]', *Madwoman in the attic*, p. 199; Webber, 'The politics of poetry: feminism and *Paradise lost*', *Milton studies XIV*, ed. James D. Simmonds (Pittsburgh, 1980), pp. 3–24.
89 Bloom, *The anxiety of influence* (New York, 1973).
90 De Man, 'Nietzsche's theory of rhetoric', *Symposium*, 28 (1974), 51.
91 Graves, *The Greek myths* (1955; Harmondsworth, 1960); *The white goddess* (1948; London, 1961).
92 Millett, *Sexual politics*, pp. 140–7.
93 Spacks, *Female imagination*, p. 39.
94 Showalter, 'Literary criticism', *Signs*, 1 (1975), 435.

4 Gynocritics

1 Trilling, 'The liberated heroine', *Partisan review*, 45 (1978), 519; cf. Amanda Lohrey, 'The liberated heroine: new varieties of defeat?' *Meanjin*, 38 (1979), 294–304.
2 Showalter, 'Feminist criticism in the wilderness', *Critical inquiry*, 8 (1981), 183; Beauvoir, *Second sex*, p. 567.
3 Friedan, *Feminine mystique*, p. 181.
4 Showalter, 'Towards a feminist poetics', *Women writing*, ed. Jacobus, p. 25.
5 Showalter, 'Feminist criticism in the wilderness', pp. 184–5.
6 See chapter 1, note 15.
7 Lakoff, 'Language and woman's place', *Language in society*, 2 (1973), 45; augmented as *Language and woman's place* (New York, 1975).

8   'Sispeak' is proposed by Stefan Kanfer (*Time*, 23 October 1972, p. 45); 'sapphistry' by Jane Marcus (*Representation of women in fiction*, ed. Heilbrun and Higonnet, p. 87).

9   Carter, 'Language of sisterhood', p. 233.

10 Daly, *Beyond God the father*, p. 153; cf. Tillie Olsen, *Silences* (1978; London, 1980).

11 Duras, 'From an interview [1975]', *New French feminisms*, ed. Marks and de Courtivron, pp. 174–5.

12 Jardine, 'Theories of the feminine: Kristeva', *enclitic*, 4 (Fall 1980), 12.

13 M–FLC, 'Women's writing', p. 30.

14 Cixous (1976) quoted by Heath, 'Difference', p. 78.

15 Cixous (1975) quoted by Verena Andermatt, 'Hélène Cixous and the uncovery of a feminine language', *Women and literature*, 7 (1979), 38.

16 Severson, 'Don't get too near the big chakra [1974]', *Spare rib reader*, ed. Marsha Rowe (Harmondsworth, 1982), p. 312; Schwichtenberg, '*Near the big chakra*: vulvar conspiracy and protean film/text', *enclitic*, 4 (1980), 82.

17 Cf. Monique Wittig, *Les guérillères* (1969; London, 1971).

18 'Woman's exile: interview with Luce Irigaray [1976]', *I&C*, no. 1 (May 1977), 64.

19 Jay L. Halio, '*Perfection* and Elizabethan ideas of conception', *English language notes*, 1 (1964), 179–82.

20 Gallop, *Feminism and psychoanalysis*, p. 29; Irigaray, 'That sex which is not one [1977]', *Language, sexuality & subversion*, ed. Paul Foss and Meaghan Morris (Darlington, Victoria, 1978), pp. 162, 165.

21 Burke, 'Irigaray through the looking-glass', *Feminist studies*, 7 (1981), 289.

22 Jones, 'Writing the body: toward an understanding of *l'écriture féminine*', *Feminist studies*, 7 (1981), 147.

23 Editorial collective, 'Variations on common themes [1977]', *New French feminisms*, ed. Marks and de Courtivron, p. 219.

24 Cf. Jane Gallop, 'Snatches of conversation', *Women and language in literature and society*, ed. McConnell-Ginet, pp. 275–9.

25 Lakoff, 'Language and woman's place', p. 48.

26 Lakoff, 'Language and woman's place', p. 77.

27 Cf. Nancie Henley and Barrie Thorne, *Sex differences in language, speech and nonverbal communication: an annotated bibliography* (Rowley, Mass., 1975), pp. 270, 272, 273.

28 Jespersen, *Language: its nature, development and origin* (London, 1922), p. 238.

29 Cf. Lucy M. Freibert, 'World views in utopian novels by women', *Journal of popular culture*, 17 (1983), 49–60.

30 Dickerson quoted by Cheris Kramer [i.e. Kramarae] in 'Women's speech: separate but unequal?' *Quarterly journal of speech*, 60 (1974), 14.

31 Kramarae, *Women and men speaking* (Rowley, Mass., 1981), p. vi.

32 Bodine, 'Sex differentiation in language', *Language and sex: differences*

and dominance, ed. Barrie Thorne and Nancie Henley (Rowley, Mass., 1975), p. 131.

33 Cf. Dédé Brouwer *et al.*, 'Speech differences between women and men: on the wrong track?' *Language in society*, 8 (1979), 33–50.

34 McConnell-Ginet, 'Review article', *Language*, 59 (1983), 384.

35 Kuykendall, 'Breaking the double binds', *Language and style*, 13 (1980), 83.

36 Woolf, 'Romance and the heart [1923]', *Contemporary writers* (London, 1965), p. 124.

37 Juhasz, *Naked and fiery forms* (New York, 1976), p. 202.

38 Annette Kolodny's version of the operative assumption in feminist literary criticism influenced by Virginia Woolf (*Critical inquiry*, 2 [1975], 76).

39 Oates, 'Is there a female voice?' *Gender and literary voice*, ed. Todd, p. 11.

40 Kristeva quoted by Heath, 'Difference', p. 79.

41 *The table talk and omniana of Samuel Taylor Coleridge*, ed. Coventry Patmore (London, 1917), p. 201; Woolf, *Room of one's own*, p. 148.

42 Cf. Carolyn G. Heilbrun, *Toward a recognition of androgyny* (New York, 1973), pp. 115–67; Nancy Bazin, *Virginia Woolf and the androgynous vision* (New Brunswick, 1972).

43 Cf. Daniel A. Harris, 'Androgyny: the sexist myth in disguise', *Women's studies*, 2 (1974), 171–84.

44 Rich, 'The kingdom of the fathers', *Partisan review*, 43 (1976), 30.

45 Mellor, 'Blake's portrayal of women', *Blake*, 16 (1982/3), 148.

46 Ellmann, *Thinking about women* (1968; London, 1969), pp. 27–54.

47 Nochlin (1973) quoted by Lucy R. Lippard, *From the center: feminist essays on women's art* (New York, 1976), p. 80.

48 Showalter, *Literature of their own*, p. 198.

49 Sexton, quoted in Juhasz, *Naked and fiery forms*, p. 141.

50 Fishman, 'Interactional shitwork', *Heresies*, no. 2 (May 1977), 99–101.

51 Woolf, 'Women and fiction [1929]', *Collected essays*, vol. 3, p. 40.

52 Spacks, 'In praise of gossip', *Hudson review*, 35 (1982), 19–38; *The journals of Arnold Bennett*, ed. Newman Flower (3 vols., London, 1932/3), vol. 1, p. 6; Cixous (1976) quoted by Heath, 'Difference', p. 79.

53 Hiatt, 'Women's prose styles: a study of contemporary authors', *Language and style*, 13 (1980), 36, 37.

54 Hiatt, *The way women write* (New York, 1977); cf. the review by Sally McConnell-Ginet, *Language in society*, 8 (1979), 466–9.

55 Hiatt, *Way women write*, p. 132.

56 Roethke, 'The poetry of Louise Bogan [1961]', *On the poet and his craft*, ed. Ralph T. Mills (Seattle, 1965), pp. 133–4.

57 Letter dated 30 June 1859, *The George Eliot letters*, ed. Gordon S. Haight (9 vols., New Haven, 1954–78), vol. 3, p. 106.

58 Ohmann, 'Emily Brontë in the hands of male critics', *College English*, 32 (1971), 909.

59 Eliot, 'Silly novels by lady novelists [1856]', *Essays of George Eliot*, ed. Thomas Pinney (London, 1963), pp. 301–24; cf. the letter to Sarah

Orne Jewett (dated 5 October 1901), *Selected letters of Henry James*, ed. Leon Edel (London, 1956), p. 234.

60   Showalter, 'Women writers and the double standard', *Woman in sexist society*, ed. Gornick and Moran, p. 340.

61   Colby, *The singular anomaly* (New York, 1970), pp. 3, 192–3.

62   Halsbrand, 'Women and literature in 18th century England', *Woman in the 18th century and other essays*, ed. Paul Fritz and Richard Morton (Toronto, 1976), p. 64.

63   Jennifer Strauss, 'The poetry of Dobson, Harwood & Wright: "within the bounds of feminine sensibility"?' *Meanjin*, 38 (1979), 336.

64   Weisstein, ' "Kinde[r], Kuche, Kirche" as scientific law', p. 236.

65   Goldberg, 'Are women prejudiced against women? [1968]', *And Jill came tumbling after*, ed. Judith Stacey *et al.* (New York, 1974), pp. 37–42.

66   Woolf, *Room of one's own*, p. 115; cf. Josephine Donovan, 'Feminist style criticism', *Images of women in fiction*, ed. Cornillon, pp. 341–54.

67   Woolf, 'Romance and the heart', p. 124.

68   Richardson, 'Foreword', *Pilgrimage*, vol. 1, p. 12.

69   Dworkin, *Woman hating*, pp. 197, 203.

70   Hanscombe, *The art of life* (London, 1982), p. 44.

71   Joyce, *Finnegans wake*, p. 203.

72   Woolf, 'Romance and the heart', pp. 124–5.

73   Amiran, 'What women's literature?' *College English*, 39 (1978), 654.

74   Lippard, *From the center*, p. 69; Heath, 'Difference', p. 103.

75   Heilbrun, *Toward a recognition of androgyny*, p. 161.

76   Hernadi, *Beyond genre* (Ithaca, 1972).

77   M–FLC, 'Women's writing', p. 31.

78   Blake, 'Pure Tess: Hardy on knowing a woman', *Studies in English literature*, 12 (1982), 700.

79   Buchan, *The ballad and the folk* (London, 1972), p. 64.

80   Eliot, 'Silly novels by lady novelists', p. 324.

81   Austen, *Northanger Abbey* (1818; Oxford, 1923), p. 38.

82   Lewes, 'The lady novelists [1852]', *Women's liberation and literature*, ed. Elaine Showalter (New York, 1971), p. 175.

83   Schreiner, *Woman and labour* (London, 1911), p. 158; Cynthia Ozick writes on 'the Ovarian Theory of Literature', in 'Women and creativity: the demise of the dancing dog [1969]', *Woman in sexist society*, ed. Gornick and Moran, pp. 309–10.

84   *Shakespeare's sisters*, ed. Gilbert and Gubar, p. xvi.

85   Moers, *Literary women*, pp. 90–110: 'Female gothic'.

86   Mussell, *Women's gothic and romantic fiction* (Westport, Conn., 1981), p. xi.

87   Kahane, 'Gothic mirrors and feminine identity', *Centennial review*, 24 (1980), 47–8.

88   Cf. Mussell, *Women's gothic and romantic fiction*, p. 16.

89   Barber, 'What if Bartleby were a woman?' *The authority of experience*, ed. Arlyn Diamond and Lee R. Edwards (Amherst, 1977), p. 223; cf.

Daphne Patai, 'When women rule: defamiliarisation in the sex-role reversal utopia', *Extrapolation*, 23 (1982), 56–69.

90 Esther K. Labovitz, 'The female *Bildungsroman* in the twentieth century, a comparative study', *Dissertation abstracts international*, 43 (1983), 2341–2; Bonnie Hoover Braendlin, 'Alther, Atwood, Ballantyne, and Gray: secular salvation in the contemporary feminist *Bildungsroman*', *Frontiers*, 4 (1979), 18–22; cf. Annis Pratt, 'The novel of development', *Archetypal patterns in women's fiction*, pp. 13–37; *The voyage in: fictions of female development*, ed. Elizabeth Abel *et al.* (Hanover and London, 1983).

91 Miller, *Heroine's text*, pp. 157–8.

92 Howe, 'Narratives of survival', *Literary review*, 26 (1982), 177–84.

93 Cf. Joyce Fullard and Rhoda Walgren Schueller, 'Eighteenth century poets: a bibliography of women not listed in the CBEL', *Mary Wollstonecraft journal*, 2 (May 1974), 40–3; '540 women poets lost to history' are listed by Jean Buyze in *The tenth muse: women poets before 1806* (Berkeley, 1980).

94 Schreiner, *From man to man* (London, 1926), p. 219.

95 Woolf, *Room of one's own*, pp. 70–5, 171.

96 Woolf, *Room of one's own*, p. 74.

97 Pratt, 'New feminist criticism', p. 176; cf. Dorothy Smith, 'A peculiar eclipsing: women's exclusion from man's culture', *Women's studies international quarterly*, 1 (1978), 281–96; Lynne Spender, *Intruders on the rights of men* (London, 1983).

98 Cf. Martha Vicinus, *The industrial muse* (London, 1974).

99 Escarpit, *The book revolution* (London, 1966), p. 34.

100 Baym, *Women's fiction* (Ithaca, 1978), p. 14.

101 Greer, 'Flying pigs and double standards', *TLS*, 26 July 1974, p. 784.

102 Moore, *Distinguished women writers* (1934; Port Washington, 1968), p. 156.

103 Spacks, *Female imagination*, p. 75; Gallop, *'Writing and sexual difference*: the difference within', *Critical inquiry*, 8 (1982), 804.

104 Barbauld in *Female spectator*, ed. Mahl and Koon, pp. 260, 267.

105 Voloshin, 'A historical note on women's fiction', *Critical inquiry*, 2 (1976), 820; cf. J. T. Frederick, 'Hawthorne's "scribbling women" ', *New England quarterly*, 48 (1975), 231–40.

106 Lerner, *The female experience* (Indianapolis, 1977), pp. xxiv–v; cf. Joan Kelly-Gadol, 'Did women have a Renaissance?' *Becoming visible*, ed. Renate Bridenthal and Claudia Koonz (Boston, 1977), pp. 137–64.

107 Letter dated 7 January 1845, *The letters of Elizabeth Barrett Browning*, ed. Frederic G. Kenyon (2 vols., London, 1897), vol. 1, p. 232.

108 Rich, *On lies, secrets, and silence* (1979; London, 1980), p. 11.

109 Mill, *Subjection of women*, p. 132.

110 *The women poets in English*, ed. Stafford (New York, 1972), pp. 22, 60–1, 82–4.

111 Jack I. Biles, 'An interview with Iris Murdoch', *Studies in the literary imagination*, 11 (1978), 119.

112 Showalter, *Literature of their own*, p. 13; on the contrasts between

'masculine' and 'feminine' traditions cf. Margaret Homans, *Women writers and poetic identity* (Princeton, 1980), pp. 12–40, 215–36.

113 Mitchell, 'From the feminine to the female', *TLS*, 1 July 1977, p. 798.

114 Gilbert and Gubar, *Madwoman in the attic*, pp. xiii, 72; Bloom, *The visionary company* (1961; London, 1962).

115 Zimmerman, 'What never has been: an overview of lesbian feminist literary criticism', *Feminist studies*, 7 (1981), 451–76; for a contrasting view see Hilary Allen, 'Political lesbianism and feminism – space for a sexual politics?' *m/f*, no. 7 (1982), 15–34.

116 Radicalesbians, 'The woman identified woman [1970]', *Radical feminism*, ed. Koedt, pp. 240–5; Wittig, *Lesbian body*, p. 9.

117 Moers, *Literary women*, p. 62.

Select bibliography

Amiran, Minda Rae, 'What women's literature?' *College English*, 39 (1978), 653–61.

Andersen, Margret, 'Feminism as a criterion of the literary critic', *Feminist criticism*, ed. Cheryl L. Brown and Karen Olson (Metuchen, NJ, 1978), pp. 1–10.

Auerbach, Nina, 'Feminist criticism reviewed', *Gender and literary voice*, ed. Janet Todd (New York, 1980), pp. 258–68.

Barnes, Annette, 'Female criticism: a prologue', *The authority of experience*, ed. Arlyn Diamond and Lee R. Edwards (Amherst, 1977), pp. 1–15.

Booth, Wayne C., 'Freedom of interpretation: Bakhtin and the challenge of feminist criticism', *Critical inquiry*, 9 (1982), 45–76.

Boyers, Robert, 'A case against feminist criticism', *Partisan Review*, 43 (1976), 602–11; cf. *Partisan Review*, 44 (1977), 111 for an editorial repudiation of some of the statements made in this article.

Carruthers, Mary, 'Imagining women: notes toward a feminist poetic', *Massachusetts review*, 20 (1979), 281–307.

Culler, Jonathan, 'On reading as a woman', *On deconstruction* (Ithaca, 1982), pp. 43–64.

Cunningham, Stuart, 'Some problems of feminist literary criticism', *Journal of women's studies in literature*, 1 (1979), 159–78.

Diamond, Arlyn, 'Practicing feminist literary criticism', *Women's studies international quarterly*, 1 (1978), 149–52.

Donovan, Josephine, 'Feminism and aesthetics', *Critical inquiry*, 3 (1977), 605–8.

  'Beyond the net: feminist criticism as a moral criticism', *Denver quarterly*, 17 (1983), 40–57.

Ellmann, Mary, 'Phallic criticism', *Thinking about women* (London, 1968), pp. 27–54.

Farwell, Marilyn R., 'Feminist criticism and the concept of the poetic persona', *Women, literature, criticism*, ed. Harry R. Garvin (Lewisburg, 1978), pp. 139–56.

Ferres, Kay, 'Since *Sexual politics*: a selected bibliography of feminist literary theory', *LiNQ. Literature in North Queensland*, 8 (1980), 101–9.

Ferrier, Carole, ' "The inadequacy of imagination": towards a feminist literary criticism', *The radical reader*, ed. Stephen Knight and Michael Wilding (Sydney, 1977), pp. 193–206.

Fetterley, Judith, 'Introduction: on the politics of literature', *The resisting reader* (Bloomington, 1978), pp. xi–xxvi.

Froula, Christine, 'When Eve reads Milton: undoing the canonical authority', *Critical inquiry*, 10 (1983), 321–47.

Gilbert, Sandra M., 'Life studies, or, speech after long silence: feminist critics today', *College English*, 40 (1979), 849–63.

Gilbert, Sandra M. and Gubar, Susan, 'Toward a feminist poetics', *The madwoman in the attic* (New Haven, 1979), pp. 1–104.

Goode, John, 'Woman and the literary text', *The rights and wrongs of women*, ed. Juliet Mitchell and Ann Oakley (Harmondsworth, 1976), pp. 217–55.

Heilbrun, Carolyn and Stimpson, Catharine, 'Theories of feminist criticism: a dialogue', *Feminist literary criticism*, ed. Josephine Donovan (Lexington, 1975), pp. 61–73.

Houghton, Greg, 'Feminist literary criticism: a critical review', *Melbourne journal of politics*, no. 11 (1979), 65–80.

'Some obstacles to a feminist aesthetic', *Melbourne journal of politics*, no. 13 (1981), 45–54.

Howe, Florence, 'Feminism and literature', *Images of women in fiction*, ed. Susan Koppelman Cornillon (Bowling Green, 1972), pp. 253–77.

Jehlen, Myra, 'Archimedes and the paradox of feminist criticism', *Signs*, 6 (1981), 575–601; cf. the responses by Elaine Showalter, Sue Warrick Doederlein, Lawrence Lipking and Patrocinio Schweickart, *Signs*, 8 (1982), 160–76.

Juhasz, Suzanne, 'The critic as feminist: reflections on women's poetry, feminism, and the art of criticism', *Women's studies*, 5 (1977), 113–27.

'The feminine mode in literature and criticism', *Frontiers*, 2 (1977), 96–103.

Kamuf, Peggy, 'Replacing feminist criticism', *Diacritics*, 12 (Summer 1982), 42–7.

Kaplan, Ann, 'Feminist criticism: a survey with analyses of methodological problems', *Papers on women's studies*, 1 (1974), 150–76.

Kaplan, Cora, 'Radical feminism and literature: rethinking Millett's *Sexual politics*', *Red letters*, no. 9 (1979), 4–16.

Kaplan, Sydney Janet, 'Literary criticism', *Signs*, 4 (1979), 514–27.

Katz-Stoker, Fraya, 'The other criticism: feminism vs. formalism', *Images of women in fiction*, ed. Cornillon, pp. 315–27.

Kennard, Jean E., 'Personally speaking: feminist critics and the community of readers', *College English*, 43 (1981), 140–5.

Kolodny, Annette, 'Some notes on defining a "feminist literary criticism"', *Critical inquiry*, 2 (1975), 75–92; cf. the responses by William W. Morgan and Beverly Voloshin, and Kolodny's reply, *Critical inquiry*, 807–32.

'Dancing through the minefield: some observations on the theory, practice and politics of a feminist literary criticism', *Feminist studies*, 6 (1980), 1–25; cf. the responses by Judith Kegan Gardiner, Elly Bulkin, and Rena Grasso Patterson, and Kolodny's reply, *Feminist studies*, 8 (1982), 629–75.

'A map for rereading: or, gender and the interpretation of literary texts', *New literary history*, 11 (1980), 451–67.

Krouse, Agate Nesaule, 'Toward a definition of literary feminism', *Feminist criticism*, ed. Cheryl Brown and Karen Olson, (Metuchen, NJ, 1978), pp. 279–90.

Lanser, Susan Sniader and Beck, Evelyn Torton, '[Why] are there no great women critics? And what difference does it make?' *The prism of sex*, ed. Julia A. Sherman and Evelyn Torton Beck (Madison, 1979), pp. 79–91.

Léger, Susan H., 'The lure of symmetry: or, the strange impossibility of feminist criticism', *Massachusetts review*, 24 (1983), 330–6.

Levy, Bronwyn, '[Re]reading [re]writing [re]production: recent anglo-american feminist literary theory', *Hecate*, 8 (1982), 97–111.

Miller, Nancy K., 'The text's heroine: a feminist critic and her fictions', *Diacritics*, 12 (Summer 1982), 48–53.

Millett, Kate, 'The literary reflection', *Sexual politics* (New York, 1970), pp. 235–363.

Moers, Ellen, 'Women's literary traditions and the individual talent', *Literary women* (New York, 1976), pp. 42–66.

Olsen, Tillie, *Silences* (London, 1980).

Pratt, Annis, 'The new feminist criticism', *College English*, 32 (1971), 872–8.
'The new feminist criticisms: exploring the history of the new space', *Beyond intellectual sexism*, ed. Joan I. Roberts (New York, 1976), pp. 175–95.

Register, Cheri, 'American feminist literary criticism: a bibliographical introduction', *Feminist literary criticism*, ed. Josephine Donovan (Lexington, 1975), pp. 1–28.

Rich, Adrienne, 'When we dead awaken: writing as re-vision [1972]', *On lies, secrets, and silence* (New York, 1979), pp. 33–49.

Robinson, Lillian S., 'Dwelling in decencies: radical criticism and the feminist perspective', *College English*, 32 (1971), 879–89.
'Who's afraid of a room of one's own?' *The politics of literature*, ed. Louis Kampf and Paul Lauter (New York, 1972), pp. 354–411.

Rooke, Constance, 'Feminist literary criticism', *Room of one's own*, 2 (1977), 40–3.

Showalter, Elaine, 'Women and the literary curriculum', *College English*, 32 (1971), 855–62.
'Literary criticism', *Signs*, 1 (1975), 435–60.
'The female tradition', *A literature of their own* (Princeton, 1977), pp. 3–36.
'Towards a feminist poetics', *Women writing and writing about women*, ed. Mary Jacobus (London, 1979), pp. 22–41.
'Feminist criticism in the wilderness', *Critical inquiry*, 8 (1981), 179–205.
'Critical cross-dressing: male feminists and the woman of the year', *Raritan*, 3 (Autumn, 1983), 130–49.

Smith, Barbara, 'Toward a black feminist criticism', *Women's studies international quarterly*, 2 (1979), 183–94.

Spacks, Patricia Meyer, 'Theorists', *The female imagination* (New York, 1975), pp. 9–41.

Spector, Judith A., 'Gender studies: new directions for feminist criticism', *College English*, 43 (1981), 374–8.

Spivak, Gayatri Chakravorty, 'Displacement and the discourse of woman', in *Displacement: Derrida and after*, ed. Mark Krupnick (Bloomington, 1983), pp. 169–95.

Stanley, Julia Penelope and Robbins, Susan J., 'Toward a feminist aesthetic', *Chrysolis*, no. 6 (1978), 57–71.

Stansbury, Sherry A., 'A bibliography of feminist criticism', *Canadian newsletter of research on women*, 6 (1977), 84–114.

Stimpson, Catharine, 'The power to name: some reflections on the avant-garde', *The prism of sex*, ed. Sherman and Beck, (Madison, 1979) pp. 55–77.

'Ad/d feminam: women, literature, and society', *Literature and society*, ed. Edward W. Said (Baltimore, 1980), pp. 174–92.

'On feminist criticism', *What is criticism?* ed. Paul Hernadi (Bloomington, 1981), pp. 230–41.

'Feminism and feminist criticism', *Massachusetts review*, 24 (1983), 272–88.

Wandor, Michelene (ed.), *On gender and writing* (London, 1983).

Whitlock, Gillian, 'Feminist literary criticism', *Women and labour conference papers*, no. 2 (1980), 557–62.

Zimmerman, Bonnie, 'What never has been: an overview of lesbian feminist literary criticism', *Feminist studies*, 7 (1981), 451–75.

Index

6684